READY TO LAUNCH

The Entrepreneur's Startup Guide

Mike A. Williams

Ready To Launch

ISBN-13: 978-1-942140023
ISBN-10: 1942140029

Published by:

Enabld Company LLC
3324 Peachtree Rd. NE, Suite 2319
Atlanta, GA 30326

Email: hello@enabld.co
Website: www.enabld.co

PRINTED IN THE UNITED STATES OF AMERICA

This guide is dedicated to:

I dedicate this book to my beautiful mother **Barbara Eason**. Mom, there aren't enough words to express how much I love you. You simply are my everything. I have been in awe of you my entire life. Through your actions, you have taught me how to love; care for others and to give generously with my time, talents, and treasures when I have been able to do so. You have helped me and my siblings be better versions of ourselves. I hope your next chapter in retirement brings you many more years of relaxation, fun, and happiness.

You rock! I love the hell out of you.

CONTENTS

SECTION 0.0
ENTREPRENEURSHIP WORKSHOP:
INTRODUCTION TO THE GUIDE

Section Goals:
- Introduce the guide.
- Provide context on the guide's approach and education strategy.

READY TO LAUNCH:

This guide will prepare individuals for the challenges that come along with starting a small business. The guide has been designed to be learned and consumed quickly. Each section will culminate with a list of questions to embed theories into memory. My hope is that this guide encourages the reader to learn more and potentially attend one of our workshops or webinars on the topic. While this guide doesn't provide the interactions with an instructor or other participants, it will provide a thorough understanding of all the basics of entrepreneurship in addition to valuable resources and tips. The guide will cover topics that include: Ideation, Capital and Cash Management, and the Business Model Canvas among others.

The three pillars of this entrepreneurship guide are education, empowerment, and execution.

Pillar I: Education: It has been said that entrepreneurship education should include skill-building components such as negotiation, leadership, creative thinking, exposure to technological innovation and new product development. We will attempt to provide as many real-world examples as possible. The education process in this guide will use the Business Model Canvas (BMC) to simplify and organize key information needed to start a business.

Pillar II: Empowerment: The guide is designed to empower and encourage readers to pursue entrepreneurial activities. It has been repeatedly shown that self-efficacy, or the belief in one's self to be able to learn and accomplish tasks, is the leading indicator of entrepreneur success. This guide's primary task is to provide the tools necessary to make an entrepreneur feel that they are adequately equipped for success.

Pillar III: Execution: This stage of the entrepreneurship guide is largely ignored by traditional teachers. This guide will specify the exact steps necessary to go from ideation to business execution, including such simple steps as building a website, creating professional emails, filing with the state revenue department, applying for a federal tax ID, getting an official looking business address, sources of capital and opening a bank account. These activities will be approached as a checklist of sorts to outline what are the minimum requirements to launch your business.

Conclusion: In short, we hope this guide will catalyze aspiring entrepreneurs to pursue their dreams and believe in their own ability to accomplish them.

This page left blank intentionally

SECTION 1.0
INTRODUCTION TO BUSINESS
GETTING STARTED IN ENTREPRENEURSHIP

Section Goals:

- Become acquainted with basic business principles and definitions.
- Define a company and business model.
- Learn the difference between a startup and ongoing business.

The critical ingredient is getting off your butt and doing something. It's as simple as that. A lot of people have ideas, but there are few who decide to do something about them now. Not tomorrow. Not next week. But today. The true entrepreneur is a doer, not a dreamer.

- Nolan Bushnell, Entrepreneur -

SECTION 1.0: INTRODUCTION TO BUSINESS

Business is a generic term that is used to describe the exchange of goods and services for compensation. This definition, which could also be described as commerce, applies to all businesses. Goods and services can take the form of either tangible or intangible goods; for example, an amazing new basketball shoe made by Nike or the services of the investment bankers at Goldman Sachs as they advise a company on financial issues. The consumers in the market determine whether a business is a success by either choosing to purchase the businesses goods & services, or not.

business

noun, often attributive business | 'biz-nes, -nez, *Southern also* 'biz-\

Popularity: Top 10% of words

Definition of BUSINESS

1.usually a commercial or mercantile activity engaged in as a means of livelihood

www.merriam-webster.com/dictionary

Whether you have an MBA or a GED, anyone can become involved in business. Have you ever seen a lemonade stand? That's a perfect example of a small business, although most lemonade stands ignore the legal, tax and regulatory consequences for legally incorporated organizations. However, most businesses start on a scale that would be considered very small compared to companies like Nike, Apple, Microsoft or Amazon. Many of today's popular brands started in a garage, or a basement, with a dream and a few dollars.

Businesses include everything from a small owner-operated organization such as a family cafe, to a large multinational conglomerate such as General Electric.

To do business with another company, a business must engage in a transaction or exchange of value with that company. A company's customers can either be consumers (B2C businesses target consumers directly) or other businesses (B2B businesses target other businesses for their goods and services). Business, as a term, can also be used to refer to a specific industry or activity. Phrases such as the "real estate business" or the "advertising business" describe industries that companies engage in commerce within.

This section will go into the most basic terms and theories necessary to understand how businesses operate.

1.1: WHAT IS A COMPANY?

Company: An organization which exchanges goods or services for revenue. A profitable company recognizes and harvests profits from their efforts.

A company is a legal entity that is set up to engage in commerce. This entity can take numerous different forms, including sole proprietorship, partnership, C Corp, S Corp, LLC, etc. These entities have strengths and weaknesses in terms of what types of businesses are best suited for each structure. For instance, if you wish to have numerous investors and many owners, a C Corp may be advisable. If you are starting a company that will be solely your own endeavor, a sole proprietorship LLC could be the best

option. When determining the structure for your business, it is a good idea to engage in legal counsel to ensure you choose the optimal structure, as the tax and administration impact of which legal structure you choose can be significant.

Interestingly, all corporations are companies, but not all companies are corporations. A *company* is a broad term that defines any entity that engages in commerce. A corporation, on the other hand, is a specific legal structure that companies have the option to choose.

1.2: WHAT IS BUSINESS MODEL?

After determining what structure your business will be, the next step is defining your business model. A business model is defined as a group of processes and functions necessary for a company to profitably operate.

Specific Parts of a Business Model: A business

has specific parts that you will need to be aware of to be successful. This section will introduce the various parts of the business model, and then come back to a more thorough review of business models in *Section 3.0 – Business Ideation.*

<u>Value Proposition:</u> This is the most crucial part of the business model, and is intrinsic to the success of your entrepreneurial hypothesis. The value proposition to your customer attempts to convince them that the item you have created is worth a certain value, ideally above the cost to produce the item. Effectively communicating this to customers via marketing, branding and other forms of communication will determine whether your business succeeds or fails.

<u>Customers – Acquire + Activate + Amaze:</u> Customers are critical to every business. They provide the revenue that you crave to grow your business. Many believe that once they connect with a customer, the job is over. However, it is important to remember that once you get in touch with a customer, the work has only begun. First, you must *acquire* the customer through a process called customer acquisition. Subsequently, you must *activate* the customer, by convincing them that your value proposition is valid and that your product is worth its cost. Activating a customer involves solid web construction for e-commerce, or well-designed storefronts for traditional retail. Finally, after your customer has made a purchasing decision, the company must *amaze* them by executing wonderful, friendly customer support or having a best in class return policy, among others.

<u>Finances – Revenues and Cost:</u> Intrinsic to the long-term success of your business is whether you can consistently turn a profit. In the early stages, if you order 100 products, the per unit cost may be higher than if you ordered 100,000. However, as an entrepreneur, you most likely do not possess the capital or risk tolerance to buy that much of an unproven product. Therefore, you must forecast the profitability for the business into the future, using sales projections, cost estimates at varying purchase levels, marketing cost estimates, and more. The financial side of entrepreneurship is simple in that it involves addition and subtraction, but complex due to the uncertainty that surrounds small businesses.

<u>Channels – Manufacturers, Sales Networks, Partners:</u> Next on the list are the partners that you choose to do business with. These can vary depending on the industry. For instance, if you start a microbrewery and produce a popular craft beer, you may need to work with a distributor to get your product into the right stores. On the other hand, a bike seat company might partner with an apparel company to build the brands of both businesses. These key channel partners must be identified during the business model formulation, and depending on how wise the decisions were regarding partners, may have a significant impact on your business.

<u>Key Activities & Resources:</u> This section identifies the key activities that must be undertaken to effectively operate a business. In the case of a marketing company, this could be producing deliverables to clients. In the case of a retail operation, this may involve interfacing with logistics, supply chain and sales channel partners. Each business is different. This section identifies the key skills and resources necessary to succeed. Simply ask the question, what does the entrepreneur contribute to the business? Guidance? Labor? These are the key activities. Key resources could be a manufacturing partner that makes the product. Each business is different.

1.3: HOW IS A STARTUP DIFFERENT FROM AN ESTABLISHED COMPANY?

A startup is very different from an established company in many ways. For one, a startup is *searching* for an opportunity to execute on. A startup deals with myriad unknowns, uncertainties and risks, so the company must be agile and able to pivot quickly to respond to market demands. Contrarily, an established company with numerous years of operation has vast amounts of data to support their decision: sales, trends, market research, etc. This allows a mature company to focus on *execution* as opposed to *search*. The skills of the support personnel necessary to operate with high levels of information (established company) are far different from the people that are best suited to operate on little to no information (startup company).

This difference in approach between startups and established companies requires a very different set of skills. Startups are temporary organizations designed to test a market hypothesis. The hypothesis is that their business model is repeatable and scalable, and the confirmation of this hypothesis can be provided by customers purchasing the business' products. Entrepreneurs must be adept at dealing with uncertainty and turning unknowns into known variables. Entrepreneurs are the people well suited to operate confidently while dealing with multiple unknowns.

 Launching a start-up, you need to get a lot done quickly. Every day is different. Everyone pitches in with everything. It's easy for the founding team to say, 'We're flexible. We all help out with everything!' But when it comes to making decisions-that flexibility can spell inefficiency and disaster.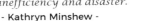

- Kathryn Minshew -

1.4: SECTION QUESTIONS

1. What is the difference between a startup and an established company?

_____

_____

_____

_____

2. What is a business model?

_____

_____

_____

3. What part of the business model deals with profitability?

_____

_____

_____

_____

4. What are the "key activities" that all entrepreneurs must perform?

_____

_____

_____

_____

5. What types of channel partners might you encounter as you run a business?

_____

_____

_____

_____

This page left blank intentionally

SECTION 2.0
INTRODUCTION TO ENTREPRENEURSHIP:
WHAT IS AN ENTREPRENEUR?

Section Goals:
- Discover what makes entrepreneurs different from other people.
- Learn about the industries that entrepreneurs operate within.
- Identify some of the daily tasks an entrepreneur may encounter.

> *Start-up success is not a consequence of good genes or being in the right place at the right time. Success can be engineered by following the right process, which means it can be learned, which means it can be taught.*
> - **Eric Ries** -

SECTION 2.0: INTRODUCTION TO ENTREPRENEURSHIP

This section will consider what exactly makes an entrepreneur an entrepreneur. To decide whether you want to become an entrepreneur, you must ask difficult questions of yourself. How do you handle risk and uncertainty? Do you believe in yourself? Can you operate on incomplete information?

2.1: WHAT IS AN ENTREPRENEUR?

An entrepreneur is a person who operates consistently at a high level under uncertain circumstances. One of the most influential definitions of entrepreneurs belongs to Joseph Schumpeter, who in 1947 wrote that entrepreneurs have a desire to "found a private kingdom, drive to overcome obstacles, a joy in creating, and satisfaction in exercising one's ingenuity."

entrepreneur

noun en·tre·pre·neur | ˌäⁿ-trə-p(r)ə-ˈnər-ˈn(y)u̇r\
Popularity: Top 10% of words

Definition of ENTREPRENEUR

1.: one who organizes, manages, and assumes the risks of a business or enterprise

www.merriam-webster.com/dictionary

Entrepreneurship is a simple mindset and process to create and develop economic activity by blending risk-taking, creativity and/or innovation with sound management, within a new or an existing organization. So, entrepreneurship can take place in a new or existing organization, although the general term *entrepreneur* applies to those who begin their own enterprises.

Operating Efficiently with Low Levels of Information – Entrepreneurs must operate with little known information, leveraging assumptions and educated guesses to make crucial business decisions

Leadership versus Management –

Entrepreneurs must be leaders, who inspire those that work for them to follow them. Entrepreneurs must also be capable managers who can run a business in parallel with motivating their subordinates to follow them. This careful balance requires charisma, leadership and management skills to pull off successfully.

Confidence and Self-Efficacy – Without self-efficacy, individuals give up trying to accomplish their goals, making self-limiting decisions that foreclose opportunities even though individuals have the necessary skills to follow a path of action.

2.1: WHO ARE THESE "ENTREPRENEURS," AND WHAT ARE THEY LIKE?

Everyone knows of the successful entrepreneurs that appear in the news: Steve Jobs (APPLE), Elon Musk (Tesla), Michael Dell (DELL), David Stewart (World Wide Technologies), and the list goes on. However, it is more difficult to define exactly what makes an entrepreneur successful. The short version is that entrepreneurs are those people who are fully obsessed with solving problems and building solutions. Entrepreneurs are some of the most resilient, mentally tough people around. Unlike employees, who barely have any risk financially or

otherwise, entrepreneurs put their entire livelihoods on the line with the belief that they can succeed.

As far back as in the 18th century Jean-Baptiste Say, a French textile manufacturer and economist, wrote that the human contribution to economic growth came in three types: scientists, workers, and entrepreneurs. Entrepreneurs generally have a habit of forming businesses in a process called serial entrepreneurship. This phrase refers to those entrepreneurs who continue to innovate, create businesses and take on risk in the face of uncertainty.

 Execution really shapes whether you company takes off or not. A lot of people start out with an exciting thing and they want to take over the world have a good plan of how to get there and the steps along the way.
- Pete Cashmore, Founder of Mashble -

What is an average day for an entrepreneur like? – Day-to-day activities of entrepreneurship include problem solving, strategic thought processes, overcoming obstacles, execution of short term ideas while balancing longer term strategies, administrative tasks, dealing with customers, supply chain management, marketing plans, blog posts, networking and more.

- **The website is down!** When you wake up in the morning the website is down. So, you need to fix the server and upgrade traffic limits to scale with the growth of your company. Involves interfacing with external technology assets or performing the update yourself.

- **The shipment is tied up in customs!** A shipment is ready at the Port of Los Angeles and you need to coordinate third party trucking services to pick up the shipment from customers and direct it to the next staging area. Involves logistics, international trade, supply chain management and communication with stakeholders.

- **One of our customers is angry with us!** An angry customer is upset that their shipment has been delayed and is destroying your company's reputation via social media. You must make the customer happy and reverse the negativity spurred by their dissatisfaction. This process can be frustrating, but dealing with unhappy customers is one of the most important roles for an entrepreneur.

2.3: TYPES OF ENTREPRENEURSHIP

- **Products & Services –** There are many ways to build a business. Generally, businesses are classified into either product or service categories.

- **Products** are tangible deliverables that can be provided for customers. Often more scalable than services, since services generally require human capital which can be costly and difficult to hire. Product examples include shoes, apparel, digital media, consumer durables, food and agriculture, and more.

- **Services** are acts that an entrepreneur performs in exchange for compensation. This could include legal services, marketing, financial, tax, audit and consulting services. These businesses are often more difficult to scale as they are heavy on *human capital requirement*, however, providing services can be lucrative and may involve less inventory risk than a comparable product company.

Sectors – Companies operate in specific industries. These industries have various requirements that may make them appealing to entrepreneurs. In general, entrepreneurs are adept at identifying market needs before larger companies are aware they exist. In this fashion, many entrepreneurs can reach market more quickly than their well-capitalized competitors. The following generalized sectors introduce the various industries that companies operate within.

- Technology: Tech is a very, very lucrative portion of entrepreneurship. Everyone wants to create the next Facebook or Twitter, so there are thousands of technology companies in this country. Technology is a very difficult sector to penetrate because of the high technical requirements necessary to create a product that has intrinsic value. These businesses are very easy to scale after creating the product, as technology deliverables are easy to provide to customers. However, the barriers to entry are formidable due to the strong competition in the industry.

• Manufacturing: Generally, if you are involved in consumer durables you will be manufacturing products for your customers. You can either purchase equipment yourself and begin to produce products as a manufacturer (high initial capital outlay) or work with someone who already has the equipment to make the products for you (low initial capital outlay) and then sell them directly to your customers. Small businesses will generally rely on these types of contract manufacturing arrangements to test out a new product before taking on the risk of production themselves.

• Hospitality & Tourism: Tourism is a great industry in some areas, and involves dealing directly with consumers who visit the area. Hotels and restaurants are good examples of businesses that rely on tourism dollars to thrive. These businesses are generally service oriented, and must be in a location that has an allure to tourists.

• Entertainment: The entertainment industry is larger than ever, and people are looking for immediate gratification when it comes to consuming entertainment. The use of technology, the internet and mobile viewing allows customers more access to entertainers than ever before. People can earn a solid living through YouTube videos, which was not possible until recently. This has led to an entirely new generation of entrepreneurs who entertain their fans and are compensated via advertisement revenue. Other entertainers include actors, singers, etc., who may or may not be true entrepreneurs.

• Professional Services: One of the largest industries in the world is the professional services industry. Entrepreneurship can take many forms, and sometimes it is as simple as an accountant leaving their day job to start an accounting company. The same can apply to investment bankers, lawyers, doctors and others. Every industry has an opportunity for entrepreneurs to carve out a niche of profitability if they can see the opportunity before them.

Risk Tolerance - In addition to the industry, different types of entrepreneurs generally possess differing risk tolerances. Take, for example, the instance of the accountant leaving his or her day job. They have taken a risk by going out on their own and starting a business. They may need to provide some capital to advertise, get an office, acquire equipment, licenses, etc. However, this situation at worst will end up with the accountant failing at their endeavor and going back to the work force.

On the other hand, someone who invested $5 million of their own money into a technology startup obviously has taken on a significantly larger amount of risk. This at risk capital can also provide larger returns than an accountant doing taxes for a variety of folks. It is crucial that you match your own risk tolerance with the risk score of your potential endeavor. If you take on more risk than you are comfortable with, you may struggle with the weight of that decision and fail to perform optimally. However, if you choose an endeavor with a risk profile that matches your tolerance, you will be far more comfortable engaging in the business activities necessary to succeed.

2.4: SECTION QUESTIONS

1. What is an entrepreneur?

_____

_____

_____

_____

2. What types of skills must a successful entrepreneur possess?

_____

_____

_____

_____

3. Name and describe an industry that entrepreneurs operate within and why you feel this industry is appealing.

_____

_____

_____

_____

4. 4. What are the two primary categories of business? Describe the difference and pros/cons associated with each.

_____

_____

_____

_____

This page left blank intentionally

SECTION 3.0
BUSINESS IDEATION:
TURNING AN IDEA INTO A BUSINESS

Section Goals:
- Discover how an idea turns into a business.
- Identify the steps necessary to review and analyze an initial idea.
- Figure out how to determine if an idea is worth pursuing.

Ideation without execution is delusion
- **Robin Sharma** -

SECTION 3.0: BUSINESS IDEATION: TURNING AN IDEA INTO A BUSINESS

Now that the fundamentals of business and entrepreneurship have been introduced, we can begin to discuss the fundamental blocking and tackling required to turn a business idea into an executable business model. Every business starts out with an idea, and 99% of businesses die before making it to the next step. Numerous successful entrepreneurs have been known to say that ideas themselves are effectively worthless; it is the execution and follow-through on an idea coupled with taking advantage of a market opportunity that produces value. This execution and follow-through is what differentiates entrepreneurs from people with lots of ideas. We all know someone who absolutely loves to talk about a vague idea they have, but never do anything to execute or further the idea. Few will approach an idea with the discipline and analytical mind necessary to move the idea from ideation to a full business model. Sometimes, they may not know how to proceed or the things necessary to pursue their ideas. In these pages, we will provide the necessary details to help you follow your dreams. The following sections will discuss best practices in business model ideation, and how you can avoid common pitfalls that many entrepreneurs face.

3.1: INITIAL IDEATION

Every idea must go through these stages, or stages similar to these, to determine if the idea is feasible. The steps involved with reviewing an idea vary, but generally center on the question, "Is this an idea worth evaluating more fully?" If the answer is still yes after challenging and questioning the assumptions the idea is based upon, then you should feel confident moving on to the next sections of business model creation. If the idea has flaws, then you may need to pivot slightly, or potentially come up with a new idea that does not have the same weaknesses.

IDEATION: Picking the Right Idea – So, how does one pick the "right" idea? There is no perfect way to ensure that an idea will be the right one. The best method is to brainstorm regularly on issues or problems you face in daily life that could be solved through a product or service. Some of the most successful ideas are simply improvements on products already being sold, so do not be afraid to piggyback off an existing product!! These are three simple steps to ideating:

1. Ideation – During step one, you are looking for quantity over quality. Any idea that comes into your head, write it down. Brainstorming like this creatively can sometimes open your mind up to new ideas you hadn't previously considered. Writing the ideas down will allow you to push them to the side, clearing space for your next great idea.

2. Synthesis – Step two will require you to cull, trim and combine your ideas to improve them. As much as step one focused on quantity, step two focuses on quality. Narrow down your brainstorming list to 2-3 ideas and move forward in reviewing these concepts.

3. Analysis and Review – Once you have culled your list down to a handful of ideas, or combinations of ideas, you are ready to ask questions and challenge the idea. Before you invest or begin a business, you must poke holes in, challenge, question

and critique your ideas with an objective, critical eye.

This steps in this list can be difficult, and some entrepreneurs assume that since they believe an idea is good, that everyone else will. This is simply not the case. We are a diverse and complicated community of people, with more differences than we can count. Thus, the perspective of a prospective customer will have an impact on their opinion of your product. Put yourself another person's shoes and attempt to understand why someone may think or behave differently, and you will be able to garner some keen insights from the process. Differences should be celebrated and embraced as much as our similarities, and the best entrepreneurs know how to see things from all their customer's various points of view.

Remember that the best ideas solve problems that customers have, or offer a solution to an existing inconvenience. This means that if you operate within a specific industry, you may have keen insights into the needs and requirements of customers in that industry that others do not. This is a great place to start when thinking of an idea. What is your background? What do you know? Is there a need in your daily life that could be satisfied by a product or service?

3.2: ANALYSIS & REVIEW

After determining that yes, this idea is worth a further investment of time, then you must move on to the analysis and review of your problem. Basically, this will involve interrogating your idea with questions designed to identify weaknesses.

Analysis: Value Proposition: In the initial review of the idea, the value proposition should be the first item you address. Can

you create a compelling value proposition for your customers? At what cost? Is anyone else currently providing this product or service? These are all crucial questions to challenge your idea.

1. Problem Statement:

- What is the problem?
- Who has the problem?

- Is it a problem people are willing to pay to solve?

2. Product / Solution:

- Why is the problem hard to solve?
- Why hasn't another company solved it?
- What key activities are necessary to solve this issue?

3. Market Size:

- How big is this problem?
- What is the potential market for customers in this area?
- Is the market permanent, or is this a temporary problem?
- How long has this problem existed, and what products and services has the market provided to attempt to solve it?

4. Competition:

- What do customers do today?
- Who is offering competing products?
- Why is your product superior?
- What part of the value proposition differentiates you from competitors, and how will you communicate that to potential customers?

5. Product:

- How do you do it?
- How is the product or service made?
- Is the process scalable and able to provide economies of scale at higher volumes?
- Do you possess the skills necessary to perform the key activities necessary to launch the product?

If not, is it a function that can be outsourced to experts?

Review: Reality Check & Back of Napkin Estimates: Once you are comfortable with your value proposition, it is important to do a quick back of the napkin estimate of costs, sales price and profitability. If you can provide a product that people are willing to pay $50 for, but it costs you $60, then you either need to find a customer willing to pay more, or find a source for your products at a lower cost. Even if these initial estimates are mostly educated guesswork, you can save a lot of time by doing a quick reality check on your idea to make sure it is fundamentally and economically viable.

Here are the five basic steps to quickly determine if your idea seems viable:

Estimate the price for your product or service (PRICE). Research competitive / similar products and determine what price point you would be willing to sell at. Determine if that price seems competitive.

6. Estimate costs for your product or service (COGS). Are they lower or higher than how much the product or service costs to provide?

7. Estimate customer acquisition cost (CAC). Is your product profitable enough to have money left over for marketing, customer service, etc.?

8. Estimate your overhead / fixed costs (OH). Do you need an office? Do you need a retail storefront? Estimate all the fixed costs necessary to run your business. Are these costs one time or ongoing? We will go into these costs, and how to conduct breakeven analysis in more detail later in the guide.

9. Subtract your costs from the anticipated sales. PRICE – COGS – CAC – OH = Opportunity. Can you make money at this endeavor? Are there any opportunities to cut costs or increase price?

Example: Feel free to keep this analysis at a very high level; if you can buy a product for $9 and sell it for $10, it will be difficult to make much money. On the other hand, if you can buy a product for $5 and sell it for $25, you have a much better opportunity for success, and a much larger margin of error to withstand hiccups. Entrepreneurs such as Tim Ferriss advocate having an 8x multiple of COGS, so if you were making a product for $5, Tim would suggest having a retail price of $40. This is tough to find, but when you can, this sort of profit margin allows you to have some flexibility in terms of your ability to grow. In short, the more profit margin available, the more significant amounts of capital you have available to spend on marketing, sales channels, new products, etc.

I knew I wanted to do something on my own, so I cam up with the idea for Silver Oak on napkins and planned the budget for the company.
- Pete Cashmore, Founder of Mashble -

3.3: PRODUCT PROTOTYPE

If you pass through your reality check unscathed, then it is time to determine how difficult it would be to bring your product to market. To do this, you must analyze what it would take to get your minimum viable product (MVP) to market. There is some guesswork involved at this stage, since you have not priced out manufacturing, human capital needs, etc., but it is a fundamental exercise that must be considered before diving into the business model. For instance, if you determine your technology prototype will cost $500,000 to develop and you do not possess that liquidity, then perhaps it is time to either find another option or a source of funding. If, on the other hand, you can get a manufacturer to make a run of 100 of your products with little trouble, then you may be able to think about launching right away.

Minimum Viable Product: The minimum viable product is that version of a new product which allows a team to collect the maximum amount of validated learning about customers with the least effort. This means you can create a product for strictly research purposes to answer the following questions:

- Will people buy my product at my projected price?

- Do customers find the product solves their issue or pain point as identified in initial ideation?

- Do customers like the product?

- Would customers recommend this product a friend?

If you determine that your product can be created in an economically viable fashion, then it is time to move on to the formal creation of your business model.

3.4: SECTION QUESTIONS

1. Create a list of potential business ideas. Write down everything that comes into your head.

_____

_____

_____

_____

2. What are the three steps of business ideation?

_____

_____

_____

_____

3. What are the five steps of business analysis and review?

_____

_____

_____

_____

4. Conduct a back of the napkin analysis for a product you would like to create. What does the product cost? How much can you sell it for? What other costs are associated with launching the product?

_____

_____

_____

_____

5. How much capital would it require to launch your MVP (minimum viable product)?

_____

_____

_____

_____

This page left blank intentionally

SECTION 4.0
BUSINESS MODEL CANVAS
BUILDING A WINNING BUSINESS MODEL

Section Goals:
- Identify and define the various parts of the business model canvas.
- Use the business model canvas to create a business model.
- Learn why each part of the business model canvas is important.

> *A business model really is a system where one element influences the other; it only makes sense as a whole. Capturing that big picture without visualizing it is difficult. In fact, by visually depicting a business model, one turns its tacit assumptions into explicit information. This makes the model tangible and allows for clearer discussions and changes. Visual techniques give "'life" to a business model and facilitate co-creation.*
> **- Alexander Osterwalder, Business Model -**
> Generation: A Handbook for Visionaries, Game Changers, and Challengers

SECTION 4.0: BUSINESS MODEL CANVAS

It's important to understand the key differences between an idea and a business model. In the previous section, we hinted at the various parts of the business model without explicitly building the entire business model. This is to save time in case an idea doesn't make the cut. However, we're now ready to take a look at the steps necessary to go from idea to execution.

The difference between a business model and an idea is that ideas are opportunities waiting to be executed, while business models provide a specific road map to execution, involve cost estimates, long term goals, market research, customer feedback and more. Business models can be very specific, providing detailed financial models, sales projections and financial statements, or they can be more general. Sometimes, the figures required

to make models and estimates may be unknown and require assumptions early in the process. Ensure that your assumptions are based on information from the market, and use the best information you have available. As you become more educated on the market and industry you're evaluating, you'll be able to replace your assumptions with more concrete estimates from market participants.

So, how do we go from an idea that we believe is potentially viable to a full-fledged business model? There are numerous ways to reach this end, but for the purposes of this guide we will leverage the Business Model Canvas (BMC). The BMC is a best in class tool used by many of the top companies and entrepreneurs in the world to evaluate business models, look for new opportunities, stimulate innovation and more.

4.1: CUSTOMERS, CHANNELS AND VALUE PROPOSITION

Customers: It should go without saying that customers are crucial to the success of your business. Many small companies fail to provide the attention to customers that they deserve. This can lead to angry customers, which will destroy value for your business more than anything else. To prevent this, adopt a customer first approach in everything you do. Consider how the customer will be impacted by changes to policy, product, branding, headcount, etc. In Section 7.2: Customer Acquisition and Retention we will discuss customer acquisition and retention, and go deeper into the profit-increasing rationale around you should want to AMAZE your customers post-purchase.

Initial Questions to Ask: Who are our customers in this market? Ages? Genders? How do we reach them? Where do they make purchases? What type of incomes do they have? How much disposable income? How do we build relationships with our customers? How will we sell to them?

Customer Relationships: Any business must be customer focused to succeed over the long term. In today's digital age, this can be as simple as sending a thank you email or providing prompt responses to email inquiries and requests.

Customer Segments: Identifying customers is a key component of any business model. Different customers have different purchasing behavior, desire different levels of service and may or may not have differing levels of income. Determining who your customers are can help you tailor your business to their needs:

• Mass Market: This approach is hardly a "segment" of the market in the most traditional sense. Contrarily, mass market brands will attempt to focus on the entire market and do not focus on specific customer segments. Think of Apple, who probably considers most people in the United States to be potential iPhone consumers. One of the reasons for the launch of their cheaper lineup of phones was to capture this market. Startups may have difficulty rising above the noise in such a large, crowded market, and the lack of economies of scale for startup organizations makes it difficult to compete from a cost perspective.

• <u>Niche Market:</u> These markets are smaller segments of the overall market, with customers that face a unique need or problem. Startups can operate more competitively in niche markets because larger competitors sometimes will disregard them as being too small to focus on. This may be a perfectly acceptable business decision for the Procter & Gambles and Apples of the world, but it presents an opportunity for an entrepreneur to fill that need. For example, Apple started as a niche company offering a new product that had very few customers in the world: The Mac Computer. Now, they have grown out of that niche into one of the largest electronics companies in the world, selling computers, tablets, phones, media devices, music, movies, and more. Start small, and work your way up the ladder; niche products are a great starting point for many startup orgs.

• <u>Segmented:</u> Often, companies innovate by "creating" or "willing" a new market. Segmentation is a preferred method for this strategy. Imagine if Apple decided that they wanted to make a superphone that only a small portion of the population could afford. It would be premium priced ($1,000+) and have amazing features. In many ways, that would segment the market between rich and regular consumers. A risk of forcibly segmenting a market is alienating existing customers if they are not receptive to the idea.

• <u>Diversify:</u> Usually more applicable to mature companies, many businesses will diversify between markets to provide more stability for their overall business.

• <u>Multi-Sided Platform:</u> Sometimes a business will serve two customer segments that are mutually dependent on one another. An example of this is credit card companies, who charge fees to merchants and provide purchasing power to credit card users.

Channels: Channels are the pathways to customers. They can take the form of sales teams, retail stores, web sites, partner stores/sites, wholesale operations and more. If you can reach a customer to make a sale, then you should consider that a sales channel. Some channels are more profitable than others, and each comes with their own strengths and weaknesses. Choosing the optimal channel for your customer group will be crucial towards your success. For example, if you decide to market to the elderly, mobile advertisements on Facebook may not be the best channel to pursue those customers. Now, if you were targeting children/grandchildren of the elderly, then perhaps this mobile/social channel could be considered. Remember to always think like your customer would think when applying the rules of the BMC.

<u>Initial Questions to Ask:</u> What channels do we expect to sell through? Are our target customers users of this **channel?** How large is the channel? How expensive will it be to leverage a sales channel? Are there barriers to selling through this channel? What type of pricing does our model suggest? Subscription? One-time purchase?

Value Proposition: The value proposition is the key component of any business model. If customers agree with the proposition that you've created value with a product, it will sell. If they deem the price too high for the value created, the business will struggle to make sales.

<u>Initial Questions to Ask:</u> What are our unique product features? Why would someone buy our product over a

competitor? What problem does our product solve? What must our customers believe to buy into our value proposition? How will we communicate the value proposition to customers?

Being self-aware, honest and objective about the value you are adding to a product can help you make business decisions around your products. The value propositions may be:

<u>Quantitative</u> – Quantified by numbers, including price, efficiency, profitability. These products possess strong calls to action with quantifiable support. They may

claim 50% fewer calories, or 33% MORE FOR YOUR MONEY. These measurements attempt to communicate to customers that, compared to other options, the product being reviewed is the best value based on the

<u>Qualitative</u> – This is more subjective measures of value-add, which can include subjective measurements, novelty of an item, newness, perceived performance and customization. The key to qualitative value propositions is that they are effectively communicated to the customer at the time of purchase.

Value Propositions

What value do we deliver to the customer?
Which one of our customer's problems are we helping to solve?
What bundles of products and services are we offering to each Customer Segment?
Which customer needs are we satisfying?

CHARACTERISTICS
Newness
Performance
Customization
"Getting the Job Done"
Design
Brand/Status
Price
Cost Reduction
Risk Reduction
Accessibility
Convenience/Usability

Customer Relationships

What type of relationship does each of our Customer Segments expect us to establish and maintain with them?
Which ones have we established?
How are they integrated with the rest of our business model?
How costly are they?

EXAMPLES
Personal assistance
Dedicated Personal Assistance
Self-Service
Automated Services
Communities
Co-creation

Customer Segments

For whom are we creating value?
Who are our most important customers?

Mass Market
Niche Market
Segmented
Diversified
Multi-sided Platform

Channels

Through which Channels do our Customer Segments want to be reached?
How are we reaching them now?
How are our Channels integrated?
Which ones work best?
Which ones are most cost-efficient?
How are we integrating them with customer routines?

CHANNEL PHASES
1. Awareness
   How do we raise awareness about our company's products and services?
2. Evaluation
   How do we help customers evaluate our organization's Value Proposition?
3. Purchase
   How do we allow customers to purchase specific products and services?
4. Delivery
   How do we deliver a Value Proposition to customers?
5. After sales
   How do we provide post purchase customer support?

4.2: KEY PARTS OF THE BUSINESS MODEL CANVAS

Infrastructure provides the backbone of any business. They involve the daily workings of the company, and can range from tangible assets and resources to key value add functions performed by employees. The three key parts to infrastructure are: key activities, resources and partnerships.

Key Activities: These are those key activities that must be undertaken by the business to create value. The "secret sauce" or determining factors that enable the company to charge a price higher than their cost of goods. These key activities are the foundation of the value proposition to your customers. The following bullets mention only a handful of the activities a company may undertake to produce value.

● *Problem solving* is necessary in all forms of business. Entrepreneurs constantly face obstacles they did not expect, and must work around these problems to succeed.

● *Supply chain management* is the management of various parts of a supply chain that, when combined, creates value for the customer. Identifying the key links in the chain, managing those relationships and leveraging them for your business is a key aspect of some companies.

● *Customer service* is necessary in almost all forms of business. To make the customer happy, you must ensure that their needs are met or exceeded.

Key Resources: Types of key resources include physical, human, financial and intellectual. Resources are necessary to prove out the value proposition.

● *Physical resources* could be equipment, buildings, vehicles and systems. Retailers rely on physical stores and must invest heavily in physical resources to reach customers. An online retailer may not own a single physical resource.

● *Human resources* are people with skills that can create value, either through a service or creating products. Human capital is crucial to service businesses, who rely on profiting from generating revenue that is higher than the amount they must compensate their human capital for their contributions.

● *Financial resources* involve the use of cash and investment to provide a return on that capital. Certain industries and businesses are more capital intensive than others. For instance, a battery manufacturer must invest heavily in a factor for their batteries, then harvest returns on the investment over time.

● *Intellectual resources* could include copyrights, trademarks or patents that can be leveraged to create value for the firm. These resources are difficult to develop, but once created can provide substantial value for firms.

Key Partners: Partners are any business that is related to, or involved with your business. They can include suppliers, customers, competitors, non-competitors, etc. This could include a manufacturer if you are creating a durable, or a technical team if you are creating software. Establishing good relationships with your partner network is crucial in ensuring long-term success for any business. The following bullets point out a few examples of key partners.

● *Strategic alliances* (non-competitors) will sometimes be formed between companies that are not direct competitors. This could be in the form of

● *Coopetition* sometimes can occur between companies that could be considered competitors. This is not to suggest that businesses should participate in market collusion or price setting, only that sometimes the combination may produce better results than the sum of its parts.

• *Joint ventures* are an example of a very formal relationship where two or more companies enter into a legal agreement to conduct a project. The details of the project can vary widely in size, industry, scope and term. Once you invest into a project with another company, you are counting them as a key partner for your business.

• *Buyer-supplier relationship* is one of the simplest and most straightforward of the partnerships shown here. If a company purchases their product from a supplier, they are relying on that supplier to perform a function. This partnership can grow over time, making it one of the key features of any business. As the relationship improves, companies can sometimes reap benefits in the form of credit, lowered costs, favorable payment terms, free shipping, and more.

Key Partners

Who are our Key Partners?
Who are our key suppliers?
Which Key Resources are we acquiring from partners?
Which Key Activities do partners perform?

MOTIVATIONS FOR PARTNERSHIPS
Optimization and economy
Reduction of risk and uncertainty
Acquisition of particular resources and activities

Key Activities

What Key Activities do our Value Propositions require?
Our Distribution Channels?
Customer Relationships?
Revenue streams?

CATERGORIES
Production
Problem Solving
Platform/Network

Key Resources

What Key Resources do our Value Propositions require?
Our Distribution Channels? Customer Relationships?
Revenue Streams?

TYPES OF RESOURCES
Physical
Intellectual (brand patents, copyrights, data)
Human
Financial

Source: Strategyzer.com

4.3: COST AND REVENUE

The financial side of the equation is not as complicated as many think for startup businesses. First, you start with a bank account, then you determine the costs for your business, and make purchases. These are known as *expenses*. Any *revenue* that comes into the business is considered revenue. To continue operating, a business must have revenues exceed expenses over the *long term*. Short term deviations can occur during recessions and unexpected business issues, but over the long term a business must bring in more than it sends out to be considered viable.

Source: Strategyzer.com

Cost Structure: Costs must be considered in any business model to remain economically viable. Estimating costs can help you tailor your business model towards the best structure for your specific market. Depending on your pricing, and whether you occupy a premium or budget position in the market, will determine how much cost you can afford to create your product. Initial Questions to Ask: What does our product cost to make? How many must we sell to break even? What is our minimum order quantity? Are there cheaper options available to create our product? If the product is a service, how much do the necessary human resources cost?

Classes of Business Structures: Determining what class your business model occupies will help you make decisions about products and pricing.

Cost-Driven – Lean cost structure that focuses on cost savings and efficiency. Cost-driven models will attempt to offer a product for a lower cost than competitors.

To participate in this market, you must possess the economies of scale to produce products at a low cost. This can be difficult for smaller companies who traditionally make smaller orders.

● Value-Driven – This model is less concerned with cost and more concerned with creating a compelling value proposition for their customers. Prices and margins in this market are generally higher due to the value being created. Most businesses that utilize this model focus on building brands and creating valuable product.

Characteristics of Cost Structures: Costs come in different forms. Fixed costs do not vary with sales growth, while variable costs do.

● Fixed Costs - Costs are unchanged regardless of sales growth (rent, subscription fees, etc.). These are known as "overhead costs" and must be paid regardless of sales volumes. Having large fixed costs can sometimes hamper the ability of businesses to adapt and be flexible. Many startups have lower fixed costs and higher variable costs to go along with sales growth.

• <u>Variable Costs</u> – These costs vary depending on the volume of production (costs of goods sold, item shipping, etc.). Generally, variable costs only increase with sales growth, and can be managed in parallel with growing revenues. For example, instead of investing in a large amount of equipment, which would be a fixed cost, small companies may leverage contract manufacturing to produce their products. This approach will increase variable costs (the manufacturer must make a profit), but will lower your fixed cost overhead.

• <u>Economies of Scale</u> – Costs can decrease as production increases in situations where economies of scale apply. Generally, manufacturing enjoys economies of scale more than services, as services require human capital and do not scale as effectively. For example, a factory may be able to offer you a much lower cost on an order of 10,000 than 1,000 but a consulting company would need to hire additional staff to increase service offerings, making the economies of scale more difficult to harvest.

• <u>Economies of Scope</u> – Costs can decrease by creating different, related products in a fashion where the production costs of the combined products are less than the individual cost of the products. A formal definition states that economies of scope provide a proportionate savings gained by producing two or more distinct goods, when the cost of doing so is less than that of producing each separately.

Revenue Streams: Revenue, or sales, are generally the first goal of any new business. Sales cover costs and validate your business model. There are numerous revenue models that are effective at <u>Initial Questions to Ask:</u> What is the source of our revenue? What are customers willing to pay for? What do they currently buy and at what prices? How do they pay? How would they prefer to pay? Where do they buy? Where would they prefer to buy? How does each revenue stream contribute to overall revenues? Is one revenue stream dominant or are there many?

• *Product/Asset Sale* – The simplest revenue model would most likely be direct product/asset sales. Selling a product or durable item to a customer directly provides control over the entire process, and visibility into growth, profitability, etc.

• *Subscription/Usage Fee* – Subscription or usage fee for "access" to some product or service. This usually applies to services or technological products. Netflix is a great example of a subscription business that has had great success.

• *Professional Services* – Charging customers for access to a service or skill that you possess, e.g., lawyers, consultants. This is another simple business model. It relies heavily on your business providing a strong value proposition to customers.

• *Licensing* – Creating a valuable item then allowing others to use it for a fee, e.g., photography, videography, music, original media, etc. Similar to a subscription fee, licensing would generally apply to specific items as opposed to accessing a suite of services/products.

• *Brokerage Fees* – Fees for facilitating a transaction or introduction between two interested business parties, e.g., real estate agents, deal brokers, etc. Brokerage fees generally rely on networking, connecting people and providing the contacts they are otherwise unable to acquire.

• *Advertising & Marketing* – Revenue from providing advertising services to a client. These arrangements are generally done based on a retainer fee plus a commission based on growth.

4.4: STRATEGIC RISK FACTORS

In addition to the key questions asked by the business model canvas, I believe you should add on a distinct analysis of the risk factors associated with the business, as well as a quick analysis of the market. If the business is too risky to justify the potential return, then you must consider whether it is advisable to pursue. If the market is too small to support a new product, perhaps you could find a way to alter your product to broaden your audience. There are always ways to pivot and shift in the face of learning more about customers, your market, and your business. The following bullets provide questions on critical risks and market analysis.

Strategic Risk Factors: What could go wrong with our business? What external factors could change our value proposition?

What sort of internal issues may prevent the business from performing? Are these risks manageable or can they potentially be completely mitigated?

A business plan must have answers to these questions, and make educated estimates when those answers are unavailable. Remember, entrepreneurs are those who are willing to face and conquer uncertainty to build a business. This means that many of the items on the BMC may not have explicit answers. Even so, the canvas provides a roadmap to the questions you need to ask and the answers you must procure. In this way, the business model canvas provides a structured approach to creating a business model that is used by businesses small and large around the entire world.

4.5: SECTION QUESTIONS

1. What type of customer does your product appeal to? Provide an educated guess of the age, income, gender, and geographic location of your customers.

_____

_____

_____

_____

2. Is your product / service cost or value driven? Do you compete on cost or provide a value to the customer beyond a simple price comparison?

_____

_____

_____

_____

3. Who are the key partners you will rely upon when launching your business? Are there risks associated with partnering with these entities?

_____

_____

_____

_____

4. Name three of the revenue streams that companies may attempt to use. What type of revenue streams does your product or service pursue?

_____

_____

_____

_____

5. What are the strategic risk factors face your business? Identify three factors and how you would overcome these risks.

_____

_____

_____

_____

SECTION 5.0
FINANCIAL STATEMENTS & BUDGETING PROCESS

Section Goals:

- Identify the three financial statements leveraged in business.
- Learn the major components of each financial statement and the ratios used to analyze them.
- Create a budget for your business after reviewing the budgeting process.

If you don't have regular and accurate financial statements, you're driving your business 100 MPH down a one-way way street the wrong way, at night, in the fog, without lights.

- Jim Blasingame -

SECTION 5.0: FINANCIAL STATEMENTS

Financial statements provide a quantifiable view of a company's performance. These statements either capture a moment in time (Balance Sheet) or look at performance over a time-period (Income Statement, Cash Flow Statement).

Many of the most important functions of business are based on the information found in the financial statements: profit and loss, taxes, solvency, credit worthiness, etc. There are many ways to create

financial statements for an entrepreneur to take advantage of. Two of the more popular options are QuickBooks and Xero.

QuickBooks has been around for many years and provides solid functionality for its users. It also produces formats that work with most tax software. Xero is an earlier stage company focused on creating financial views for entrepreneurs and small business easily and effectively.

5.1: INCOME STATEMENT, BALANCE SHEET & CASH FLOWS

The three financial statements are: income statement, balance sheet and cash flow statement. All are important in different ways and measure various aspects of the business' condition. For example, the income statement deals with revenues, expenses and profits/losses. It provides a view over a period like a month, quarter or year. The balance sheet, on the other hand, gives a snapshot of debt, assets and equity

on a given day, such as December 31st.

Income Statement: The income statement reports on a company's financial performance over a specific accounting period, such as a year, month or quarter. This summary statement combines expenses and sales to reach profit. The income statement is also known as P&L, or profit & loss.

The purpose of the income statement is

simple: to show whether the company made or lost money during the period being reported. This information is incredibly important to shareholders, managers and creditors. The primary sections of the income statement are defined below:

Revenue: Cash inflows for rendering services or delivering product to a customer are known as revenues. This is the most basic aspect of the income statement, as is referred to as the "top line" and sales revenue.

Expenses: Expenses are those cash outflows necessary for conducting business. Advertising, marketing, legal assistance, office supplies, utilities, rent, accounting work, etc., are all examples of expense categories. Knowing how much you will spend on these items is crucial to knowing how much you must charge a customer to turn a profit.

Cost of Goods Sold (COGS): COGS are the direct costs of creating a product. This includes materials, overhead for production and direct labor costs. Direct

labor is the labor associated with creating the product. For example, a worker at the factory where your product is made would be direct labor, but a sales associate selling the product to customers would be indirect, as they did not help create the actual product.

A completed income statement is shown to the right. As you can see, expenses generally rise as a business grows, but profits can be attained so long as top line revenue increases commensurately.

In this example, you can see a variety of expense categories that you might want to consider using for your budget in the next sections. These are the same account categories that you will use to project your budget forward.

The next section will go over financial ratios in more detail. For now, notice the two ratios included in this view: gross margin and net margin. These are basic financial ratios that are used to determine how efficient a company is at creating profits. These margins vary by industry and company stage.

Michael Williams Entrepreneur Advantage Workshop
Completed Income Statement

	Actual 2013		Actual 2014		Actual 2015
Revenues:					
Sales	325,000		375,000		425,000
Cost of Goods Sold (COGS)	100,000		110,000		115,000
Gross Revenue	**$**	**225,000**	**$**	**265,000**	**$ 310,000**
Gross Margin %	*69.2%*		*70.7%*		*72.9%*
Expenses:					
Advertising	5,000		10,000		15,000
Bank Fees	500		750		750
Accounting	2,500		2,500		3,000
Insurance	1,000		1,000		1,500
Legal & Professional Services	1,500		2,000		2,500
Licenses	1,000		1,500		2,000
Office	500		1,000		1,000
Rent	15,000		17,500		20,000
Salary	55,000		65,000		75,000
Travel & Entertainment	2,500		2,500		3,500
Utilities	2,500		3,000		3,500
Miscellaneous	7,500		7,500		10,000
Total Expenses	**$**	**94,500**	**$**	**114,250**	**$ 137,750**
Earnings Before Tax (EBT)	130,500		150,750		172,250
Taxes	45,675		52,763		60,288
Net Income	**$**	**84,825**	**$**	**97,988**	**$ 111,963**
Net Margin %	*26.1%*		*26.1%*		*26.3%*

Next is the balance sheet.

Balance Sheet: The balance sheet analyzes the company's capital structure at a given point in time. This generally happens both quarterly and annually, although smaller companies may choose to only produce a balance sheet at year end.

A standard company balance sheet has three parts: assets, liabilities, and ownership equity. Assets are tangible things the company owns that have value. This could be inventory, buildings, factories, etc. Liabilities are debt that the company must pay back to some third party. This could include a loan or outstanding bill from a vendor.

Assets and liabilities can be either current or long term. Current assets / liabilities are those that have maturities of less than one year; for example, a six-month loan is an example of a current liability. A current asset example would be cash in a money market account.

Ownership equity is the difference between assets and liabilities. Think of equity as all the value the business has created over time. Positive equity is necessary to continue operating unless additional investments are made. If you owe more than you own, your business may have negative equity and could face insolvency if something isn't done to make up for the difference. If you are facing negative equity, additional investment or strong profits can help you recover.

Creating a balance sheet involves amortizing debt and creating a capital structure, so building one from scratch

is not as straightforward as an income statement. It also doesn't provide any forward-looking insight, since the balance sheet represents only a moment in time. The best way to create a balance sheet for your company is to use accounting software like Xero or QuickBooks.

Cash Flow Statement: A cash flow statement looks at all cash flows over a given accounting time-period. It also shows how changes in balance sheet accounts and income affect cash. For example, if you increase sales but none of your vendors have paid, you might see a large increase in Accounts Receivable (A/R), which would represent a current asset on the balance sheet instead of revenue. This can help you determine how many of your sales are flowing through to the income statement and turning into actual revenue. The cash flow statement has three sections: operating, investing and financing activities.

Operating activities are the exchanges necessary to operate the business on a day to day basis. This includes inventory changes, receipts for sales, payments to vendors, etc. '

Investing and financing activities include operations that larger companies engage in more than small companies. An example of an investing activity would include the sale or purchase of tangible assets or fees related to a merger. Financing activities include dividends, net borrowing and activities related to financing the company's operations.

5.2: INTRODUCTION TO FINANCIAL RATIOS

Financial ratios turn the data in financial statements into useful information. Ratios can be used to compare financial statements of different companies. Each

financial statement has ratios associated with it, but the income statement and balance sheet are the most commonly analyzed statements. Here are some examples of financial ratios and what they are used for.

Net Margin (Income Statement): Net margin, also known as profit margin, is calculated by dividing net income by revenues. Net margin represents how much after tax profit you earn on each dollar of sales. This can be used to compare companies in the same industry to see if one is more efficient at turning sales into profits.

Gross Margin (Income Statement): Gross profit margin, also known as gross margin, is calculated by dividing gross profit by revenues. A company requires adequate gross profit to cover operating expenses such as SG&A and advertising. In the income statement above, you can see a gross margin of ~70%. This is a very healthy gross margin for most industries.

Current Ratio (Balance Sheet): The current ratio is simply current assets divided by current liabilities. A company wants this ratio to be more than one, since it is a goal of companies to have more current assets than current liabilities. If this ratio is below one, a company may have trouble finding the capital to meet their short-term obligations.

Debt to Equity Ratio (Balance Sheet): Debt to equity is calculated by dividing liabilities by equity. The debt to equity ratio is designed to measure how leveraged a company is. If a company takes out too much debt, it is known as being "levered." While this can increase profits, it also increases the risk that a company will fail.

5.3: CREATING A BUDGET

Creating a budget is an incredibly important part of business planning that many entrepreneurs fail to consider. When creating a budget, you must make assumptions on what your future expenses will be based on incomplete information, so some estimating must be done.

To create a budget, use a blank income statement and your knowledge of what expenses will be. Fill in the various holes using assumptions based on market information you have gathered, such as how much it will cost to manufacture your product. You can either apply percentage escalators to historical figures, or create the budget from scratch leveraging assumptions. Early stage businesses will depend more on the latter, since they lack historical figures to base projections on

Escalators: If you have an existing history of income, you can also apply escalators to increase your expenses by a percentage amount. In the view below, you can see that we are assuming each category to

grow by 10%.

In the income statement and budget on the next page, you can see that we increased sales by 15% a year, and expenses by 10%. This is because we're assuming some efficiencies and economies of scale from growing as a business. You can see this difference in sales and expenses reflected in the financial ratios include; net and gross margin both increased during the budgeted time periods by ~3%.

Category Based Budgeting: As opposed to simply applying a percentage escalator, you can also choose to project each expense category independently, which takes more time but could be more accurate if you have good information on future costs and expenses. If you know exactly how much COGS will be at each level of production, then you can apply those levels to your budget as you expect to reach them.

If you plan on spending X amount on

advertising, then you can simply plug that number into the budget and keep track of whether your over or underspending.

Conclusions: When budgeting, ask whether the assumptions seem reasonable and as you get more information on sales and expense trends, make sure to update the budget accordingly. Do you believe profitability will increase as the company grows? Where will these benefits come from? Lower COGS? Less advertising needed because of repeat customers? There are countlessways to analyze future state operations, and using solid assumptions is the first step in building a reasonable budget.

Michael Williams Entrepreneur Advantage Workshop

Income Statement with 2016/2017 Budget

Revenues:	Actual 2013		Actual 2014		Actual 2015		Budget 2016		Budget 2017
Sales		325,000		375,000		425,000		488,750	562,063
Cost of Goods Sold (COGS)		100,000		110,000		115,000		126,500	139,150
Gross Revenue	$	**225,000**	$	**265,000**	$	**310,000**	$	**362,250**	$ **422,913**
Gross Margin %		*69.2%*		*70.7%*		*72.9%*		*74.1%*	*75.2%*
Expenses:									
Advertising		5,000		10,000		15,000		16,500	18,150
Bank Fees		500		750		750		825	908
Accounting		2,500		2,500		3,000		3,300	3,630
Insurance		1,000		1,000		1,500		1,650	1,815
Legal & Professional Services		1,500		2,000		2,500		2,750	3,025
Licenses		1,000		1,500		2,000		2,200	2,420
Office		500		1,000		1,000		1,100	1,210
Rent		15,000		17,500		20,000		22,000	24,200
Salary		55,000		65,000		75,000		82,500	90,750
Travel & Entertainment		2,500		2,500		3,500		3,850	4,235
Utilities		2,500		3,000		3,500		3,850	4,235
Miscallaneous		7,500		7,500		10,000		11,000	12,100
Total Expenses	$	**94,500**	$	**114,250**	$	**137,750**	$	**151,525**	$ **166,678**
Earnings Before Tax (EBT)		130,500		150,750		172,250		210,725	256,235
Taxes		45,675		52,763		60,288		73,754	89,682
Net Income	$	**84,825**	$	**97,988**	$	**111,963**	$	**136,971**	$ **166,553**
Net Margin %		*26.1%*		*26.1%*		*26.3%*		*28.0%*	*29.6%*

5.4: SECTION QUESTIONS

1. What's the difference between the income statement and the cash flow statement?

2. Which statements are based on a period and which statements are designed to be a snapshot of a moment in time?

3. What statement are net margin and gross margin based on? What do these ratios attempt to accomplish?

4. What are the two ways you can create a budget? Which do you prefer and why?

5. Use what you've learned to create a basic budget for your company. What are the hardest categories to project? How did you reach your assumptions?

SECTION 6.0:
FOUNDING A BUSINESS
STEPS AND CONSIDERATIONS

. . . .

Section Goals:
- Identify the steps necessary to found a legal business entity.
- Understand the tax and liability implications for each legal entity.
- List out the administrative tasks necessary to found your business.

. . . .

> *Starting a company is like eating glass ans staring into the abyss. If you feel like you are up for that, then start a company.*
> - Elon Musk -

SECTION 6.0: FOUNDING A BUSINESS

Once you've determined what form your business model should take, it is time to get down to the crucial details of launching a business. To conduct business, you must determine the legal structure, source of financing and how you will process transactions (get paid) and interact with your customers.

6.1: INCORPORATING A BUSINESS

The process of incorporation can be simple, but there are many different considerations you must make. To start a business, you must register it with the Department of Revenue in your state. Prior to launch, you'll also need to apply for a business license with your city or county. The process of starting a business is often complicated, so the Georgia Secretary of State recommends that you consult an attorney or accountant as you create your business plan.

In certain districts, you'll first need to appropriate a state tax identification number, a trade name registration and potentially a zoning approval for your business location (if you have a physical location). Additionally, you may need to apply for corporate registrations, professional licenses or other special operating permits prior to application.

When you're ready to start your business and to find out more about business licensing in your area, you should make an appointment with your local Chamber of Commerce or development authority.

List of items you may need to complete:

- Federal Tax ID (EIN)
- State Tax ID
- Business licensing from city/county
- Business registration from state
- Zoning registration for physical locations
- Organizational documents (Articles of Incorporation/ Organization, Operating Agreement, etc.)
- Corporate Bylaws

- Non-Disclosure Agreement

- Online Privacy Policy / Terms of Service

To ensure you meet all required laws and policies, it is suggested that you engage with a local attorney.

Questions to Ask When You Incorporate: It is important to be strategic in your decision making when incorporating your business. You must decide, at this point, whether you want partners, what sort of liability protection you desire and how to approach business taxation. These are complicated affairs, so working with a CPA or attorney can be useful at this point of the process. Some early questions you might ask include:

Should I Take on a Partner? This is a personal decision that has pros/cons based on each specific case. When considering whether to take on a partner, consider the following:

- Does the partner perform any of the key activities necessary for the business to perform? Are they crucial to the value proposition?

- What sort of relationship do you have with the partner? Have you worked together before? Are your risk tolerances similar?

- Has your potential partner engaged in entrepreneurship before? Are they aware of the risks and uncertainties associated with starting a small business?

- If the relationship was ruined, would it be something you would regret? Many times, business relationships can go south, so it is important that you avoid putting stress on a relationship you are not willing to sacrifice.

There are numerous pros and cons to the structure you choose for your business. The list includes sole proprietorship, partnership, LLC and corporation.

Sole Proprietorship – A Sole Proprietorship involves one person, one director and one owner of the company. This structure is best suited for people who do not believe they do not need additional investors or owners. The person and company are indistinguishable in the case of a sole proprietorship, and this means the owner is responsible for both the profits and debts of the company. Pros: Easy to set up, total control over the company, taxes are simple to file, most common legal form.

Cons: Unlimited liability, you are responsible for any debts from the business, unable to bring in investors without restructuring, large burden on the owner of the company.

Partnership – A partnership involves more than one owner, and comes in several forms: General Partnerships, Limited Partnerships and Joint Ventures. General partnerships usually assume that profits, liability and management duties are shared equally amongst the owners. If there is an unequal split, this must be defined in the partnership agreement. Limited partnerships allow partners to have limited liability as well as limited input with management decisions. Sometimes limited partnerships are advisable for shorter term projects. Finally, joint ventures act in much the same way as a general partnership, but only for a limited period of time or for a single project. If the two parties continue to work together, they must file paperwork to that end.

Pros: Easy to file, shared powers and financial commitment, potential for complementary skills amongst partners and provides a partnership incentive for employees.

Cons: Joint and individual liability, shared profits, potential for disagreement amongst partners.

Limited Liability Company (LLC) – A limited liability company is one of the most popular entity structures for new businesses. The LLC a hybrid legal structure that provides the limited liability features of a corporation and the tax efficiencies and operational flexibility of a partnership. A LLC allows for limited liability for the owners, which shields their personal assets from the company in case things do not go well.

<u>Pros:</u> Limited liability, easy to create and administer, can be taxed as an S Corp, shared profits amongst owners. <u>Cons:</u> Limited term as the LLC is usually dissolved when a member leaves the entity. Self-employment taxation.

Corporation (Inc.) – A C Corp is a traditional legal structure for companies that allow greater flexibility when raising funds, working with investors or going public. The C Corp is held legally liable for their business dealings, and shareholders are protected from any liability. This provides protection for shareholders that may not be involved in the day to day decisions of the company.

<u>Pros:</u> No liability for shareholders, ability to raise capital through unlimited shareholders in the company, corporate tax treatment which generally provides lower overall tax rates for the company's profits.

<u>Cons:</u> Difficult to administer, potential double taxation of dividends and bonuses.

These structures provide pros and cons for an aspiring entrepreneur. If you are starting a small business, the most common structure will most likely be a sole proprietorship or LLC if you are working with others. The decision basically depends on whether you wish to have liability shielding (LLC) or if you are comfortable being responsible for all your businesses liabilities (sole proprietorship). Before making any decisions, be sure to speak with legal counsel.

6.2: TAX CONSIDERATIONS

Taxes should be considered within the context of your financial situation. The following section will provide a brief introduction to business taxation, and what you should know before you start your business. The Small Business Administration (SBA) states that the effective tax rates for small businesses when it comes to federal income taxes average from 13.3% for small sole proprietorships to 27% for small S corporations. The marginal total federal corporate tax rate in the United States is 35% at the federal level and 39.2% once state taxes are accounted for, per the 2013 OECD Tax Database. The global average is much lower, at 25%. Some developed countries, however, have taxes that are much higher. Always confer with legal counsel or certified accountants when considering options for tax treatment.

- What are taxes?
  - ▸ Description of business taxes in the United States
  - ▸ Key dates and information necessary for business owners

- How do I pay business taxes?
  - ▸ Ways to pay business taxes, similarities to personal taxes

- Are business taxes separate from personal taxes?
  - ▸ Depends on the legal entity. Corp vs LLC vs proprietorship

6.3: ADMINISTRATIVE TASKS

When setting up your business, it is important to get your house in order prior to product launch. This means having a web presence, emails, phone capabilities, accounting, etc., set up so you can focus on running the business when it launches. The following bullets go through some of the administrative tasks that are crucial to being successful in entrepreneurship.

Although these may seem like common sense items, they are neglected by many entrepreneurs in favor of focusing entirely on marketing, advertising or product development. Without the proper structure, a company with an amazing product can struggle to scale.

• Internet – To run a virtual office, first you need access to the internet. If you don't have internet, there are many places with free Wi-Fi that you can go to get some work done. Public libraries are some of the best places to work, as they sometimes have private rooms and the quiet necessary to be productive.

• Website - Every business needs a website in the 21st century. Your URL, or web address, will become your calling card. Now, it is easier than ever to create a website with almost no technical skills required

▶ Do it Yourself - Leverage a site like GoDaddy to register, host and create a website on one account. You can use a template for the site or install an industry standard like WordPress so you can choose themes from across the internet.

▶ Outsource It – If you don't want to mess with it, then you can get a freelancer on Upwork.com to create you a very simple website for a very reasonable cost.

• Emails - Every company should have professional emails that have your business name in the URL. When you set up a website, make sure to add on an email account that you can use for business. Nothing says amateur more than receiving a business quote request from flychick69@yahoo.com. Don't do it.

• Phone Service - If you don't want to use your personal telephone to communicate with customers, there are numerous options available. Some are free, but many require small per minute charges. You can even get a brand-new number for your business, for little to no cost.

▶ VoIP – Any general voice over internet protocol (VoIP) service will allow you to make calls over the internet.

▶ Low cost cell phones – Now, it is very easy to acquire a low-cost cell phone with basic telephone capabilities. This may be a good option if you will be operating your business while traveling, or if you are constantly on the go.

• Office Capabilities – You will need to be able to print, scan, fax, etc., as many businesses still require signatures and approvals via fax. This can be done with a variety of technologies, and most all rely on the internet. If you get an all-in-one printer, you can connect it to a wireless internet hub and have printing, faxing and scanning available, all for less than $200.

• Benefits – You will need to consider benefits if you are starting a business that may have employees, or if you would like to acquire insurance and benefits for yourself. Benefits are tax deductible for businesses, so it is a smart cash management decision to get health insurance through your business. Changes to health insurance laws has made it easier than ever for entrepreneurs to get access to affordable care. We've included several startup benefit options for small companies in Exhibit A: Resources for Entrepreneurs

- <u>Accounting</u> – Accounting is important for your business, and can be easily outsources to a tax professional. Many businesses offer cost-effective accounting services to small companies. We've provided a list of vendors for accounting services to startups in *Exhibit A: Resources for Entrepreneurs.*

6.4: SECTION QUESTIONS

1. What are the four types of legal entities that are available when founding a business?

_____

_____

_____

_____

2. Which legal entities provide liability protection for founders?

_____

_____

_____

_____

3. What statement are net margin and gross margin based on? What do these ratios attempt to accomplish?

_____

_____

_____

_____

4. What are the two ways you can create a budget? Which do you prefer and why?

_____

_____

_____

_____

5. Use what you've learned to create a basic budget for your company. What are the hardest categories to project? How did you reach your assumptions?

_____

_____

_____

_____

SECTION 7.0:
IDENTIFYING THE MARKET:
CUSTOMER VALIDATION AND ANALYSIS

Section Goals:

- Learn why customer research is imperative to running a successful business.
- Discover various ways to research your market and customers.
- Determine how your product meets or exceeds customer expectations.

Don't find customers for your products, find products for your customers.

- Seth Godin -

SECTION 7.0: IDENTIFYING THE MARKET

Once the steps provided in the previous sections are complete, it is time to launch your business officially. After registering with the state and federal authorities, you will be able to open a bank account, provide the initial investment in the company and begin engaging in commerce.

Currently, the business model created in Section 4.0: Business Model Canvas is unproven. You have made assumptions based on research, but now must validate those assumptions in the marketplace. Once you're able to validate the hypothesis that customers are willing to pay for your product, and that your value proposition is valid, you can begin to market your product and make sales. First, you must find customers on a limited basis to ensure that your business model is viable.

7.1: CUSTOMER IDENTIFICATION & VALIDATION

The BMC will provide you with details of who your typical customer might be. Now that those customers are identified, you must target them and acquire them for your business.

Customers: To validate your business model, you must determine if the customers listed on your BMC exist and behave in the manner you anticipate. If you assume a customer will make a purchase decision based on a product and projected price, and they do, then you will have success. However, if you are incorrect that customers find your value proposition valid, there may be issues

finding customers in the market. In this case, you may need to pivot / adapt by offering your product at a lower price, changing your sales channel or altering the product to make it more attractive to customers. The two steps in this are discovery customers and validating their interest in the product or service.

Customer discovery: This process takes the vision of the founder and translates it into an executable hypothesis about a business model. At this point, the effort is spent on discovering whether a customer for this service or product exists. If, after surveys, investigation and research, you decide that these customers do exist, then you move on to the validation of those customers. Here are some tools to identify customers and discover who would be interested in your product:

- Market Research: Research into the market can provide confirmation of your assumptions about your customer group. Market research can be conducted by the entrepreneur, or can be outsourced to professionals. One clever way to acquire market research is to take on the role of one of your customers; using the sales channels you have identified, look for similar products on the market place and price them out. Be objective in your comparisons of the product to your own, and realize when a product might be considered superior. This sort of direct market experience will help you live a moment in the shoes of your customers, and better understand how they may find your business.

- Surveys: Surveys will give you an idea of the mood of your customers, and how successful your value proposition is at compelling them to make a purchase decision. Surveys allow you to try different methods, prices and strategies to see which one your customers prefer. Surveys can also be unreliable, because some customers may respond to a survey in a different way than they might respond to a product in the market.

Customer validation: This process takes the potential customers we discovered in the previous step and tests whether customers will purchase the good or service. This proof of market concept helps determine whether the resulting business model is repeatable and scalable. If not, you return to customer discovery to potentially pivot the item or service into something more desirable, more efficient, or somehow otherwise improved.

- *Proof of Concept Already Exists in the Market:* There is a potential that similar products are already being offered in the market. If you are expecting your product to cost less than a competitor's product and your product offers similar or superior benefits, then this may be enough to convince you that the market demand is real. There is a chance, however, that even though you may believe that a market opportunity exists based on research into competitors, that your own product may not fare as well. Things that could contribute to this are well-entrenched market incumbents, brand loyalty issues, etc.

- *Limited Sales Rollout:* Another idea is to make a small run of your products to ensure that demand exists for them. Instead of making 5,000 products, you might do an initial run of 100 and then try to sell them via your BMC identified sales channels. This is the most thorough way to evaluate a market, as the customers will be purchasing the product and not just marking yes in a survey when asked if they would buy the product.

7.2: MARKET ANALYSIS

Market Type: What type of market is it? There are many different types of markets, and they must be targeted very differently. Determining the type of market you are operating within can prevent your business from making mistakes and judgment errors.

- Clone Market: Clone markets attempt to duplicate the efforts, nearly identically, of another successful business or enterprise. This leads to increased competition and, in general, downward pressure on margins. Look for competitors doing the exact same thing you are doing to determine if your business is targeting a clone market. An example of a clone market would be creating fashion t-shirts with clever slogans and sayings on them to market online. Numerous companies have been successful at this, and your business model could, in many ways, be identical to theirs. However, the key activities necessary to succeed involve unique shirts, clever design and other activities that may make your offerings more attractive than competitors. Understanding just how capable your team is at performing these key activities when compared to the general market can give you a good idea of your chances of success. Another example would be a CPA offering accounting services to small businesses. This service business is already replicated around the world, but the entrepreneur may believe that he can perform the service more effectively, or offer a differentiating factor to get a leg up on existing competitors.

● Niche Market: A niche market is any market that is only subscribed to by a small portion of the general population, or those with very specific needs or desires. For example, there may not be many professional cyclists, but their requirements on equipment are so substantial that there are companies that only sell a few hundred bikes a year, yet reach millions in revenue. Niche markets are usually more premium priced objects that may be difficult to create or find customers for. An example of a niche market would be aftermarket car parts or wetsuits for deep sea divers. These items are not appealing to the wider market, but may be incredibly interesting to the right demographic. Improvements in technology and social media have enabled companies to target specific niche markets better than ever. Leveraging these tools will be crucial in finding the exact customers that you niche business requires.

● Resegmented Market: This refers to a market that has been recently shuffled or made different either by regulation, company interference/innovation, or numerous other causes. In a resegmented market, there may be a new opportunity to provide a product or service, but generally incumbents will react quickly to market resegmentation due to their intricate knowledge of those markets. A market may be resegmented due to the actions of market participants, introduction of new regulations or laws or a change in consumer behavior. Identifying these trends early on will enable you to take advantage of them and create value for your customers.

● New Market: Creating an entirely new market for a company is inherently difficult to validate, and riskier than participating in mature, established markets. The rewards are also much higher, and creating a new market may provide your company with a significant first mover advantage as well as high growth. A good example of a new market player is Apple. They created the iPod, iPhone and iPad when people were not even entirely sure that they needed such items; now these items are as indispensable as the landlines were in the decades prior.

Market Size: Determining the size of your entire opportunity can provide insights into how aggressively you should pursue your launch. If you believe that your market is quite large, and that there are few market operators who can offer the services or products you are launching, then it might be a good idea to pursue this market aggressively to build market share. This could involve forgoing profits in the interest of sales growth. If you are operating in a small market, it might be a better idea to focus on repeat buyers and providing above average service for your customers.

The following questions can help you determine how large your market is, and how you should move to penetrate the market post launch.

• Volume: How many products do you estimate are sold a month in your sector? How many are sold a year? How many do you think you could sell in each period? How many do you need to sell to cover your costs?

• Revenue: What are the total revenues for your industry? What portion of those revenues do you have access to through your anticipated sales channels? What amount of revenue do you realistically believe you can acquire for your business? What would be considered a success?

• Growth: Has the market grown recently, or is it in decline? What stage of the product life cycle are your products in?

• Available Research: Do large companies operating in your sector provide research on the market through annual reports or materials made available to shareholders? Are there any reports available from market / industry experts that could help you learn more?

Product life cycle stage: It's important to know what point of the product life cycle stage your industry is in. Depending on the stage, you may have success battling existing companies.

• Introduction – In this stage, a product is just being offered to a select group of early adopters. This product has not been widely proven and significant risks remain. Companies are generally losing money at this point to test a prototype or service. For example, in the introduction stage, there will be more competitors but they will have shorter tenures in the market since it is so early in its life stage. This means that customers will still be determining

who to give their hard-earned dollars to, and brand loyalty will be low. Later in the stage, customers will have established preferences and brand loyalties which can be incredibly difficult to overcome. Profits in the introduction stage are non-existent, as market operators compete with one another to gain customers and prove out their respective market hypotheses.

• Growth – At this point, many of the questions and challenges facing items in the introduction stage have been successfully overcome. Customers are no longer considered early adopters, and sales are increasing rapidly. Growth is increasing and at some point in this stage many companies will go from losing money to breaking even. Profits are tempered by increasing scale of production and required investments to meet the needs of an ever-increasing customer group. Risks in this stage involve scaling operations, hiring staff necessary to grow and dealing with a growing base of customers. A good example of an industry in the growth stage would be electronic watches, which have launched within the past few years and are not yet a mature market. Numerous market participants have come and gone in this market, and it seems it will be dominated by a few well-capitalized companies (Apple, Samsung, etc.). Now that we have several generations of watches to review, customers who are not considered early adopters are entering the fray. These models will continue to improve their products, innovate, grow operations and eventually reach profitability in the maturity stage.

• Maturity – At this point, the product is a known quantity and sales growth begins to slow. During this stage, it is possible for companies to make reliable amounts of money on selling products. Often, these industries are known as cash cows because of the profits companies can harvest in a well-established, known market. Many companies in the maturity stage attempt to resegment the market and create a new, related product that they can a) charge more for or b) create for less money when growth declines and sales slow. Without innovation, products eventually go from maturity to decline. An example of a mature market that may face decline is the traditional computer market. Laptops and desktops have been around for decades, and now are faced with increase competition from more mobile solutions like iPhones and tablets. To persevere, laptops now come equipped with touchscreens and long battery life to compete with the smaller mobile options. Companies who traditionally operated within traditional computing have resegmented the market to include tablets, and have begun offering tablets themselves to combat declining computer sales. Being able to innovate is crucial to avoid the decline stage.

- Decline – During decline, sales growth

may stall or become negative. Technology may be presenting more efficient alternatives and replacements for our product, rendering us closer and closer to obsolescence. Companies either innovate a new product before/during this stage, or they face significant challenges. Many companies may decide to use the cash generated in the maturity stage to diversify into other, higher growth businesses. Even if an industry is in decline, the process is long and arduous and companies are still capable of making revenues on the way down. Larger, more efficient companies generally fare better near the end of the life cycle, as their diversified earnings streams are better able to withstand the challenges of declining sales in one division. A good example of a market in decline is the computer printer / scanner market. The more advanced technology gets, the less we rely on paper. Many companies have gone "paperless" and avoid printing vast amounts due to the negative environmental association.

7.3: CREATING THE PRODUCT OR SERVICE

The process of creating a product is far more straightforward an example than a service company, in terms of providing a useful example of how to create something. In the services industry, a lawyer will act very differently from an accountant, who will have different priorities than an advertising agency.

Generally, people must have experience in a market before they can purport to offer professional services. After all, the definition of a professional is someone who is paid for their services; if you have never participated in an industry, it is unlikely that customers will be willing to compensate you for your service. Therefore, this section will focus primarily on product creation, but the lessons and strategies can be useful when applied to

your specific service industry. The steps to launching a durable product are as follows:

1. *Research Manufacturers in Your Industry:* Finding the right method to manufacture your product is crucial. You must find the right partner to help you reach commercialization. Some manufacturers are more likely to work with small companies than others, so you must find someone willing to start small and grow alongside your business.

2. *Choose Appropriate Manufacturers:* After researching the manufacturers available, find several options for creating your product. Things to consider during this phase are the expertise and experience of the manufacturers, culture, communication style and comfort with the staff of the manufacturer. It is wise to trust your instincts at this point and ensure you choose a strong partner.

3. Identify the Product Specifications: Depending on how technical your product may be, you will need to provide specific requirements to the manufacturer. Most manufacturers will work with you to determine these specs, and assist you in providing the detail necessary to create a product.

4. Request Quotes from the Identified Manufacturers: After identifying the specs of your product, it is time to determine your order size. Some manufacturers have minimum order quantities, so finding a manufacturer willing to produce the number of products you desire is important.

5. Choose the Most Appealing Quote and Place an Initial Order: Once you have received the quotes from your selection of manufacturers, it is time to decide and place an order. Things to consider during this phase are price, payment terms, experience of the manufacturer and comfort with their staff.

6. Receive the Product and Begin the Sales Process: Once you receive your products, you are ready to take the next step towards launching your business. This involves sales, marketing and advertisement, which will be covered extensively in the Section 7.0: Marketing & Promotion.

7.4: SECTION QUESTIONS

1. What business cycle stage does your product or service currently occupy?

_____

_____

_____

_____

2. How large is the market for your product?

_____

_____

_____

_____

3. What strategies can be used to gain information on the customers in your industry?

_____

_____

_____

_____

4. What category of market does your product reside within?

_____

_____

_____

_____

5. What are the steps to create a product or service? Which step do you think will provide your largest challenge?

_____

_____

_____

_____

This page left blank intentionally

SECTION 8.0:
MARKETING & PROMOTION :
CREATING A COMPELLING BRAND

Section Goals:

- Learn the basics of naming & branding and why they are important to your business.
- Learn about the acquire, activate, amaze strategy for customer acquisition and retention.
- Become familiar with modern traffic generation and growth hacking strategies.

> *Branding is the promise, the big idea, the expectations that reside in each customer's mind about a product, service or company. Branding is about making an emotional connection.*

> — Alina Wheeler —

SECTION 8.0: MARKETING AND PROMOTION

Marketing and promotion are critical for growing a small business. Getting your product in front of prospective customers can be difficult, but with the right approach to branding, small companies are better able to compete than ever before.

Large consumer product companies are coming under increasing pressure from small brands with rabid followings. Take, for example, KIND Bars, a company founded in 2004 by Daniel Lubetzky. KIND has gone from a one-man operation to a company with 500 people in about ten years. They have challenged the existing ruling class of consumer products, the Procter & Gambles of the world, and created a profitable niche by providing products that people want.

How do you become the next KIND Bar? You must brand your product effectively, work hard at treating every customer as a potential opportunity to build a relationship and offer a product that people love.

8.1: NAMING AND BRANDING

More than ever, naming is important in a world where information overload is the new norm. Our brains are constantly assaulted by new brands, new products and new advertisements that target our human psychology to convince us to make a purchasing decision. To stand out from the myriad products that we see every day, your product name should be something you spend a fair amount of time discovering.

Naming Guidelines: To successfully build a brand, you must choose a name that is compelling and in sync with your story. There are many considerations to make when considering a name:

<u>Easy to Understand:</u> You just have a few

seconds to make an impact on your customers. When the name appears, it must be compelling and in line with your product. Think about your value proposition and how your name might emphasize or highlight the unique aspects of your product. The easier the name is to interpret; the faster customers will recognize what you are offering and determine whether they are interested in the product. However, your name must also be unique enough to differentiate from competitors and perform well in search. This balance is difficult to achieve, but crucial to the long-term success of the business.

Arbitrary & Fanciful: Many of the best brands in the world have no meaning other than the being a descriptor for their business. Google, Facebook, Twitter, Uber. These brands took a word and created something more. This also helps these companies in terms of their appearance in search results. When a person searches for "Twitter," there is very little doubt what site will come up first. If they had chosen a name that was not unique, they could face competition from similarly branded products. The unique nature of a name can be a potent brand defense.

Brand Story: KIND Bars have a mission: a small business spreading kindness throughout the world. It's succinct, straightforward and provides a strong connotation with the name of the brand itself. This is a compelling brand story. To create a brand story for yourself, you must ask yourself what your brand represents and what your goals are for your business. If you are interested in giving back, then highlighting your philanthropic efforts can be additive to your brand. The following points illustrate the value of a brand story.

What is your brand story? Having a brand story is crucial to creating a successful business. To have a brand story that is in lock step with your product, you must know your customers. During customer validation, get as much information as possible on your customers so that you can cater your brand story and messaging to them directly. What are their interests?

• *Local company story* – Leverage the fact that you are a local business owned and operated by an entrepreneur to endear you to customers. There is an increasing trend away from large, faceless organizations in favor of smaller businesses. People are much more likely to purchase your product if your CEO is accessible via Twitter, for example. It's a lot easier for a startup CEO to interact with every customer than the CEO of a multi-billion-dollar organization. Use this to your advantage, and show your customers that you are a person who is interested in their welfare and happiness.

• *Premium product story* – Convince your customers that your product is the best, and that it is almost an honor for them to purchase it. This sort of "club" behavior can have an incredible impact on a purchaser's decision to buy. If they are convinced that purchasing your item will improve their ranking within social circles, then you have an advantage over other, less coveted items. Premium products must live up to the hype, so be careful not to brand a budget product as premium, or be prepared for unhappy customers.

• *Socially conscious story* – Often, people will prefer brands that have a philanthropic or socially conscious tilt, all else being equal. What forms can this take? The options are myriad. Something as simple as donating 5% of your sales animal welfare, or to combat child trafficking, can be enough to convince customers that not only will they get a high-quality product, they will be supporting humanity at the same time.

<u>Why is your brand story compelling?</u> Knowing your customers will be crucial in determining if your brand story Know how they feel about certain social issues, so you can refrain from supporting issues that may upset your customers.

Ensure that your brand story meshes with your actual product. A company selling bullets may not be able to effectively support a gun control lobby without appearing hypocritical. Also, customers of a bullet company are not likely to find that sort of philanthropy additive. Instead, you could donate to a firearm safety foundation or provide ammunitions to law enforcement to show that you support our public servants. There are many ways to build out this brand story, and the process will be crucial to creating long term value for your business.

8.2: CUSTOMER ACQUISITION AND RETENTION

Customers must be fought for, guarded and tended to, before and after a sale. To build a business model that is sustainable over the long run, one must take care of customers before, during and after purchase. Some companies focus on finding customers, but then fail to close the sale. Many companies focus on finding customers and selling to them, but then neglect the process of follow-up and customer service. To succeed, you must acquire, activate and continually amaze your customers.

1. ACQUIRE – Customer acquisition is known to be a crucial driver of sales growth. To acquire a customer, you must get their attention through the noise of all the other marketers attempting to do the same. Customer acquisition methods will depend heavily on what channels you are leveraging to build your business. It could take the form of a sales network, distributor, direct sales through search results, Amazon.com marketing, and more.

Human psychology plays an important role in how advertisements are structured. Simple changes to wording can have a profound impact on the effectiveness of your campaigns. Working with experienced marketers can help you optimize your offerings and target the customers you need to grow. The following strategies represent the 21st century evolution of marketing:

Customer acquisition is directly correlated to the amount of traffic and impressions you can make upon prospective customers. Further discussion of methods and strategies to find customers will be discussed in the next portion of this guide, *Section 7.3: Traffic Generation.*

2. ACTIVATE – Activating customers can be more difficult for some companies than others. Oftentimes, a company will have a product or service that is so compelling that getting the customers there is more than half the battle, the sale might make itself. In other categories, it may take far more aggressive selling practices to take this customer from inactive to fully activated (i.e., a purchase). Levels of competition, competitor offerings, type of purchase and price of the product all contribute to the ease with which a customer can be activated.

Take for instance two companies, one that sells automobiles and one that sells seat covers. The automobile manufacturer operates through dealer networks, and requires a large capital investment to make a sale. Cars are generally the second highest purchase a person makes in their life, after their home. It will take considerably more effort, therefore, to convince someone to purchase a $25,000 automobile, than it would to convince them to buy $49 worth of zebra-print seat covers. The marketing approach is entirely different depending on the channel and value proposition you provide to customers. Things that influence activation:

Knowledge of Your Customers: Engagement throughout the lifecycle isn't just about the value you can cultivate from your relationship with the customer - it's also about the value you can deliver to your customer. A McKinsey & Company survey discovered that creating engaging and sustainable customer relationships is the top priority for Chief Marketing Officers, even more than bottom line results. This illustrates the importance of understanding your customers, meeting or exceeding their needs, and following up with best-in-class customer service.

Identification of Digital Behavior and Personas: Technology allows us to market to the most specific demographics we can imagine. If you are interested in targeting only Hispanic female amputees over the age of 70, you can do so. That market may not be large enough to build a business off of, but others will be! Determining how your customers operate on digital platforms will be increasing in importance for the foreseeable future. Knowing customer demographics can tell you who your customers are, but identifying their behavior can help you better understand their desires and needs. Ways to harvest value from identifying digital behavior include web site optimization and targeted advertising.

In terms of personas, this is another example of "putting yourself in the customer's shoes." Simply create various customer personas from your market research. How old are your customers? Where do they shop? What do they like?

Who do they get their information from? How do they make purchasing decisions? Creating an imaginary persona can help the process become more tangible; instead of thinking about customers abstractly, you'll be able to point to specific personas when deciding how to market.

Identify customer stage and speed: Decide which stages you want to drive customers to, and which stages you want to ensure customers avoid. In other words, are customers getting stuck in stages you want to move them out of quickly? For example, do customers become dormant for a year after their first purchase? How can you keep customers engaged even if they're not making a purchase?

3. AMAZE – Acquisition and activation are the only two steps you need to generate sales. However, it would be folly to treat your existing customers as anything other than a crucial cog to building recurring revenue. Recurring revenue is a revenue source that reliably occurs repeatedly over time. Many service contracts and subscription services utilize a recurring revenue model. If you offer a subscription, a major priority will be to ensure that these customers are very happy so they don't feel the need to cancel the service. If you offer a product that is a one-time purchase, you will find that customers who have already purchased the product will be some of your greatest assets. If you ensure these people remain happy, they will increase sales through word of mouth, social shares and more. Turning these first-time purchasers into brand advocates is one of the most crucial steps in building a long-term, sustainable business.

So, how do you turn customers into brand advocates? To *retain* customers and foster repeat buying behavior, further touches are needed on the customer. These customer service touches will vary depending on your customer demographic and their preferences, but may include:

• *Email Follow Up* – Getting in front of negative reviews or publicity can be as easy as sending the customer an email after purchase to ensure all their needs were met, and to offer to remedy any situation that is taking away from their positive buying experience. It is a careful balance, however, as many people may view emails like this as spam, regardless of your good intentions. Make them short, to the point, professionally designed and offer a carrot to the customer for reading the email; this might include a coupon code or something free for the customer.

• *Hand Written Cards* – In the digital world, many are reverting to old-school, hands-on techniques to differentiate themselves with customers. Hand-written cards can be attractive, especially to the older demographic. There are even companies that will have someone hand write your cards and send them out for you. This, as well as many other entrepreneur resources, is included in Exhibit *A: Entrepreneur Resources.*.

• *Phone Call Follow Up* – Phone calls are tricky, because depending on the age and temperament of your customer demographic, your customers may simply hate talking on the phone. If your customers are older individuals who are not savvy with the internet, you may want to try to reach out to them through the more personal, traditional telephone method. However, if your customers are teens, you may have better luck with social media or the internet. Again, understanding your customers is key to understanding what customer retention policies to follow.

8.3: CUSTOMER ACQUISITION AND RETENTION

Generating traffic to your business can be difficult. The arena is crowded with competitors, and making your brand stand out above the noise can prove to be quite complicated. Modern technology allows companies to be incredibly targeted with their marketing efforts, which can allow you to compete with larger competitors.

Content Generation – Search engines love original content. Too many companies attempt to copy content, create mass content, or flood search engines with content continuously. The best way for a startup to gain traffic remains creating original content that users find *interesting and valuable*. This could be motivational images, relevant quotes, original blog posts, interviews with industry experts, links to relevant content, etc. To drive traffic, the information you create must *provide value* that is not already being provided. How *valuable* the content you put out via your marketing channels ends

up being, is dependent on how well you understand your customers and their needs.

Search engines pay special attention to social links and shares by your customers. They indicate that a customer finds your content valuable enough to share with their personal network. Growth hacking, explained below, leverages this share heavy movement to enable you to build traffic through social, affiliates and other means.

Growth Hacking – Part of the acquire stage of marketing, growth hacking is the practice of losing low-cost, highly targeted technologies to quickly, cheaply, and efficiently generate traffic for your business. Growth hacking is defined a process of experimentation across different marketing channels to identify the most efficient, effective ways to grow a business. Growth hackers are marketers, engineers and entrepreneurs that focus on building and engaging the user base of a business. Ryan Holiday's book, "Growth Hacking" is an excellent resource for any aspiring entrepreneur. More useful resources are listed in *Exhibit A: Entrepreneur Resources.*

• *Social Focus* – Social media presence is crucial for any business to successfully operate. People love to have direct access to the internal workers of a company, and since people spend their days glued to their mobile phones, social media offers a convenient, familiar way for them to interact. When you combine this with the fact that quality social signals (shares, comments, likes, traffic, etc.) has a positive effect on SEO, and it is a no-brainer.

• *Pay vs Share* – You must decide whether you wish to engage in a traditional paid marketing program to generate clicks through cost per click programs, like Google Adwords or Amazon Sponsored Ads, or whether you want to leverage the power of social to increase shares, likes and social signals. These can be run in parallel, but different businesses may receive different ROIs from these channels based on their customer demographics.

• *Partner Sites / Affiliate Linking* – Often, businesses will set up partnerships to share one another's content to access new customers. This could take the form of a joint charitable event, exchange of

blog posts, links to one another's websites, etc. These partnerships can create value for both brands, and help the companies grow.

Traditional SEO – The process of SEO involves optimizing your web site to show as high as possible within search results on Google and other search engines. It is crucial to the long term rank your website will have in search that you analyze your pages and blog posts, and optimize them based on SEO best practices. You may choose to outsource this function or perform it yourself.

• *Outsourced* – To outsource this function, you must source a freelancer experienced with SEO. You can find affordable freelancers on sites such as UpWork and Fiverr, who will help your SEO process at an affordable cost.

• *Insourced* – If you believe you can perform the function yourself, there are a wide variety of books and online resources to help you optimize your site. If you operate a WordPress website, there are numerous plugins and tools to enable Google Analytics, search optimization, keyword focus and more. Using these tools, you can effectively optimize your website, but experts in the industry may be more effective at it. You must decide whether hiring an expert is worth the additional cost to your business.

8.4: SECTION QUESTIONS

1. Define brand in one sentence.

_____

_____

_____

_____

2. In your own words, why is brand important and what aspects of brand do you find compelling?

_____

_____

_____

_____

3. What are the types of brand stories? Which type of story do you find most compelling?

_____

_____

_____

_____

4. Describe the ACQUIRE + ACTIVATE + AMAZE strategy. How would you perform these functions for your product or service?

_____

_____

_____

_____

5. What are the parts of growth hacking and why is it important to startups?

_____

_____

_____

_____

This page left blank intentionally

SECTION 9.0:
SOURCES OF CAPITAL & CASH MANAGEMENT STRATEGIES

Section Goals:

- Learn about the sources of capital, including the costs and benefits of each.
- Identify the various types of capital available to entrepreneurs.
- Discover best practices in cash management and how they can help your business.

 It's not the return on my investment that I'm worried about; it's the return of my investment.

- Will Rogers -

SECTION 9.0: SOURCES OF CAPITAL & CASH MANAGEMENT STRATEGIES

When starting a business, not everyone possesses the capital necessary to get off the ground. Sources of capital are more available than ever, and depending on your level of risk tolerance and general outlook, certain options are sure to be more appealing than others.& Gambles of the world, and created a profitable niche by providing products that people want.

How do you become the next KIND Bar? You must brand your product effectively, work hard at treating every customer as a potential opportunity to build a relationship and offer a product that people love.

9.1: SOURCES OF CAPITAL

Sources of capital come in many forms. The following general types of capital are available to entrepreneurs:

Friends & Family: One of the most popular forms of early stage funding is friends and family. A large majority of startups leverage this type of funding in the early stage. The benefits are obvious: friends and family are already known to you, usually have less stringent requirements on reporting than more sophisticated investors and generally are invested in you as a person and hope you have success. The risks of combining family and friends with business are also substantial. Many friendships and family relationships can be strained when money is involved, and the inherently risky nature of startups exacerbates this.

Angel Investors: Early stage investment is also done on a grand scale by angel investors. These are generally wealthy individuals or funds designed to invest in only very early stage companies.

Angel investors will require more in the way of business plans and supporting information than family and friends. They are also capable of providing significant professional counsel and support as you grow your business, which can be invaluable to inexperienced entrepreneurs. The risk is that they are not invested in your as a person and view the transaction in a strictly business context.

Startup Incubators: Incubators are great options for entrepreneurs. They offer workspace, funding, professional advice and connections in the industry. Incubators sometimes charge companies to use their services if they do not require funding or take a small equity portion as part of the arrangement. This means you can sometimes get connections, funding and workspace at one location. Incubators generally have time limits on how long a company can be in development, so if your company takes too long to grow, an incubator may be forced to remove you from their portfolio or start to charge you for the workspace.

Small Business Administration (SBA): The SBA is a government funded organization that provides capital funding to businesses with at least two years of historical operations. This can be a great option for a young business that has a short history of performance. The paperwork and regulatory reporting requirements of the SBA provide considerable headaches for entrepreneurs, so only pursue this route if you understand the work required to receive funding.

Credit: Credit cards are available to entrepreneurs relatively easily. The ease of acquiring a credit card and ability to use the card for a wide variety of expenses is appealing to entrepreneurs. However, if the company goes under the entrepreneur is generally liable for any debt they incur due to the personal guarantee the credit card requires. This can be a considerable risk.

Small Business Loans (Non-SBA): Non-SBA loans are more available than ever. Vendors such as Kabbage provide funding to small companies very quickly. Risks include strong requirements in the loan documents and the ability of a company like Kabbage to put a lien on your company if you fail to pay.

As an entrepreneur, you must decide which source of funding is appealing to you.

9.2: TYPES OF CAPITAL

The sources of capital above include debt and equity. In this section, we'll take a look at these types of funding and the pros and cons associated with each.

Debt: The most straightforward option, debt is simply cash you borrow and pay interest on until it is repaid. The more debt you acquire, the more highly leveraged your company becomes. In the case of a downturn, debt can be crippling to a company. Most financial crises were the result of abundant debt. While riskier than equity since you must pay it off, debt allows you to keep 100% control of your company and not have additional investors who may not agree with how you manage the company.

Equity: Ownership in the company, or equity, is investment that you do not need to pay back. Equity investors buy a portion of your company and are then tied to you until the equity position is bought out. In some cases, equity investors remain investors until an exit situation presents itself for the company. Some investors prefer to get out before this happens, so understanding the time line an equity investor is operating on is important.

Hybrid Offering: Some options may present a combination of equity and debt. For example, convertible debt options could be presented to a company in the form of debt, and if the company performs well the lender could have the option to convert that debt to equity. This provides the lender with a higher upside, which make them more willing to invest.

9.3: CASH MANAGEMENT STRATEGIES

Factors that contribute to cash management include a company's liquidity, management of cash balances and short term investing strategies. In many ways, cash flow management is the most important role a business manager undertakes. Here are three best practices for managing cash flows as a new business manager.

Use Technology to Shorten the Cash Conversion Cycle (CCC): Technology allows companies to perform cash management functions more effectively than ever before. While it may have taken a month to get an invoice out by mail to a vendor twenty years ago, there are now tools that can allow you to send an electronic invoice the same day. If your payment terms are a certain amount of days after the invoice is received, this can make a huge difference in your cash levels.

Visibility – Cash Flow Reporting: Like we mentioned above, financial statements are crucial to providing visibility on how healthy your company is. To know your cash situation, you need to create reports based on real numbers. Tools like Xero and QuickBooks can be incredibly useful. Once you have a view on your cash flow situation, it's time to optimize your approach to cash flow management.

Optimize Processes: After you've created your projections and reports on cash flows, it is time to optimize your processes. Taking a keen eye and looking at how fast you are paid, how fast you pay vendors, etc., can help you realize where there are holes in your cash flow processes. Negotiating more favorable payment terms on receivables and payables can help you balance. Additionally, implementing the technologies mentioned above can help solve issues that the cash flow reporting uncovers.

9.4: SECTION QUESTIONS

1. What sources of capital were most appealing to you as an entrepreneur? Why were these options appealing?

_____

_____

_____

_____

2. What are the risks associated with friends and family investors? How are these risks different than angel investors?

_____

_____

_____

_____

3. What is the difference between debt and equity? Why would you prefer one over the other?

_____

_____

_____

_____

4. How can technology help you improve your cash management?

_____

_____

_____

_____

5. Is cash management an important function for business managers?

_____

_____

_____

_____

SECTION 10.0:
EXIT STRATEGY:
BEST PRACTICES FOR A PROFITABLE EXIT

Section Goals:
- Learn about the process for selling or exiting a company you own and operate.
- Identify best practices for preparing your company for a profitable exit.
- Determine the questions that need to be asked prior to beginning an exit process.

I've never believe you should start a company to sell it. You start a company to solve a problem and do something cool. You sell it based on how the markets are doing and how the industry is doing -- you can't plan this. Find a good set of advisors who you work well with and can give you great advice.

- John West, Serial Entrepreneur -

SECTION 10.0: EXIT STRATEGY

Many entrepreneurs have no plans to ever exit their investment. However, sometimes an entrepreneur may start a company with this goal directly in mind. Many technology companies will attempt to prove the concept of their product, and then immediately look for a large company to acquire them and allow the product to quickly scale. Others will engage in grassroots efforts to build the business before selling it off.

Exit strategies are important to consider if you are interested in exiting your company at some point. It is important to know that certain legal structures make investment more easy, while others require a restructure that can become costly. Discuss with your legal advisor the impacts of the type of legal entity you have chosen on your ability to raise funds.

IF you are interested in an exit, the following pages will discuss the various aspects of the exit process, including pre-exit positioning, creating a best in class pitch, and the exit process itself.

10.1: POSITIONING YOUR COMPANY FOR EXIT

To position your company effectively to be bought, you must understand the needs and desires of potential acquirers. In addition, you need to focus on building a company that someone wants to buy rather than one you want to sell. There can be quite a difference between the business you want to run, and the types of businesses people want to buy.

For instance, while you personally may want to avoid a certain sales channel like retail due to the lower profitability and increased hands-on management, many buyers will require that you have multiple sales channels or a national presence before they will consider you for acquisition. Understanding exactly what matters in your specific industry, through research and discussion with other market participants, will be critical in helping you prepare for an exit.

In addition to making a company that someone wants to buy, you must focus on making a company that would be easier to buy than build. Create real value, and don't take shortcuts. "Acquiring synergistic and complementary products or solutions can create significant value for the acquirer." notes Eric Rosow, Chairman of ReadyDock and president of Scry Health. "They look at the opportunity to get into new markets or acquire new customers that the buyer may not have any relationship with. The buyer may not have a presence in a particular market or with certain customers, but that could be improved by acquiring another company's products, people and customers."

Common Reasons for Exit – The reasons for exit can vary based on the industry environment, state of the economy and health of the business, but generally fall into the following categories:

● Retirement of the primary shareholder

● Competitive pressures

● Death or illness of the owner

● Financial difficulties

● Readiness of heirs to take control of the business

● Realizing value

Determining what the catalyst is for the exit can help determine the optimal structure for a deal. For instance, if a founder wishes to retire, one option would be to allow his employees to purchase shares in the company. This ensures that incentives are aligned, and that the people who helped build the company can benefit from its continued success. If competitive pressures are hampering the ability of the business to compete, however, then a more drastic measure may prove necessary.

Key Questions to Ask Prior to Exit – Selling your business, into which you've poured your heart, soul, sweat and tears, can be an incredibly difficult decision. To reach the right conclusion for you personally, you must ask yourself tough questions.

● What is important to me in life? Do I want to continue running this business or do I want to begin a new journey?

● Why would I want to keep the business in the family? Who relies on this business that I care about?

● What are my financial needs? Do I have a need for liquidity?

● How important is it to maximize the monetary considerations I receive, relative to other aspects of the deal? Would I accept non-cash considerations? Am I looking for a big payday, or a removal of risk?

● What kind of management role, if any, would I like to have in the business? For how long? Could I imagine a situation where I'm no longer involved in the business?

● How do I decide whether to retain a financial stake in the business? What ownership level would be acceptable to me?

● Who do I want to sell or transfer the business to? How do I choose among family members, employees, financial investors, competitors, or others? Who do I think would be willing to purchase the business?

• What managerial expertise is required for my business to continue to be successful? Who is willing and able to run the business? What preparation do they need to take on that role? Will the business be successful without me?

• What can I do to protect or reward my employees or others with a stake in the business? Are there employees who would be dissatisfied by an acquisition? Have I been forward with them about our potential options?

• What other motivating factors might affect my decision? How do I feel about the business keeping its name and identity following my exit? Is it okay if it is absorbed by a larger brand?

• How important is it that my business retains its independence? Do I believe the business would benefit from becoming part of a larger organization?

How should the business be structured and financed to take advantage of future opportunities? Do we require financing at present? Does an acquisition prevent future financial hardship? These questions must be answered to provide a full picture of your stance on exit. Some people may believe that an exit is an attractive idea, but after discussing it with employees or advisors, may have a change of heart. It is important that you make a decision that is right for you and not one pressured by externalities, stakeholders or investors.

Key Value Drivers - Value drivers are the real and perceived aspects of your business that can enhance the value received for your firm. To receive a premium on book value, the business must have created a repeatable and sustainable model to create future value. Sometimes, a company may have invented a product that has intrinsic value in and of itself. Other times,

a brand name or loyal customer base may have a perceived value. Revenues and sales growth are associated with higher valuations. Common value drivers include:

• Intellectual property: patents, trademarks and brand

• Quality and reputation of your business

• Customer relationships

• Growth trends for key products and services

• Distribution network

• Cash flow and profitability

• Technology related assets

• Quality and depth of your management team

• People and intellectual capital

• Synergies expected from a merger / acquisition

These items add to the value of your business and must be considered when determining how to prepare your pitch. You must focus on the key items that show your firm is worth acquiring, while also being honest about the shortcomings and weaknesses of your business. In addition to key value drivers, you will need to identify competitive threats, weaknesses in the market or business model, risk factors and other negative potential outcomes to the business. If an acquirer does their proper due diligence, these facts will come to light eventually, but it is much more efficient to be upfront and honest about any holes in your defense. Acquirers will appreciate the candor and it will save time and effort during due diligence. Being misleading about numbers, sales or any material aspect of your business can lead you down a dark path that will end in disappointment.

10.2: BEST PRACTICES FOR PITCH DELIVERY

Pitches are made all over the world in a variety of settings. A *pitch* is basically an effort made by a group of people to reach a desired end. This could be a pitch to offer advertising services, or a pitch to acquire a $4 billion oil conglomerate. Business relies on these efforts, and if you are starting a service business, you will be required to repeatedly pitch new customers on your services. In order to be taken seriously, you must create a high quality pitch deck and accompany it with solid presentation skills and analytical support. The following bullets cover some critical aspects of successful pitch delivery.

• *Concise* – Many entrepreneurs love their businesses. The harsh reality, however, is that the people you are pitching to will not provide you with a standing ovation no matter how long and detailed your pitch is. Generally, you are in front of busy people who want to receive information in the most efficient and effective way possible, so that they can decide. Some entrepreneurs make the mistake of creating 100-page pitch decks and business plans that people simple do not have the time or patience to read. Thus, concise pitching is of utmost importance. Focus on creating a book that effectively communicates your major points as quickly as possible. Try to think of whether each word is necessary and how to deconstruct complex ideas into manageable factoids. If you overwhelm your audience with words, the message will be lost in the noise.

• *High Level of Polish and Design Work* – If you are not a designer, or familiar with creating pitches, then you should strongly consider hiring a professional to assist you with your pitch. This sort of assistance doesn't have to break the bank!! There are tons of capable professionals that would enjoy helping you with your pitch via UpWork or other freelance sites. Be sure to create a pitch that is highly polished, well designed graphically and provides a professional representation of your business to potential investors. Err on the side of spending *too much* time on your pitch; after all, you've spent years building up your business and an exit is one of the most important parts of realizing the value from those efforts.

• *Reviewed by Multiple Parties* – Be sure to engage with a third party to review the pitch for grammar, design, logical progression, completeness and tone. Often, after staring at a document for weeks on end, it can become difficult to see glaring errors or changes that should be made. To this end, engage in third party support for review of your pitch. Best practice is to give your pitch to someone familiar with the process so they can critique not only the pitch deck itself, but also your presentation skills.

• Encompasses Specific Ask and Supporting Information – If a potential investor has specific asks for you prior to the pitch, ensure that they are adequately represented in the materials. There is nothing worse than having an interested party make requests, only to receive a non-customized presentation that only contains what the entrepreneur feels is relevant. Investors are careful, calculating and require the supporting information for statements made in these presentations. Ensure that all your statements adequately represent fact, and that you can provide the detail behind statements if necessary. Best practice is to have the data at ready should any questions arise.

Find more information on the best practices of pitch making in *Exhibit A: Entrepreneur Resources.*

Types of Pitches: While this section is

focusing primarily on exit pitches, there is a need to produce other types of pitches during the normal course of business. The following bullets list out several common types of pitches that you may need to engage in, depending on the nature of your business.

- *Customer Pitch* – In some businesses, you might be pitching your services to customers in person. This would apply to financial services, consulting, marketing, legal, etc. In these situations, your focus in the pitch should be on *how you solve your customer's needs.* Support these assertions with statistics and facts that adequately represent your business, and do not overstate your capabilities.

- *Vendor Pitch* – Some vendors may want to know something about your business strategy or plan to ensure that you are a capable business to work with. When engaging in vendor pitches, focus on financial and credit metrics to assure the vendor that you are a viable partner. Sales growth, strong accounting policies and adequate liquidity are strong considerations for vendors.

- *Investor Pitch* – When looking for investment, the process will almost always involve a pitch deck and supporting materials. Investors will be more thorough than any other potential stakeholder when interviewing you and analyzing materials. For this reason, it is suggested that you look for external help when raising capital.

Creating an Exit Pitch Deck: Now that you have a basic understanding of the considerations necessary to create a pitch, we'll discuss some of the components of a pitch and why they are crucial.

- *Introduction to the Business* – Introduce your business and its primary products and services. This should include a brief overview of growth, revenue and profitability to provide a foundation of information that can be reinforced later in the pitch.

- *Financial Snapshot* – Most investors will be most interested in the financial health of your organization. Companies that seek investment during negative performance will see a commensurate decrease in valuation from potential investors, due to the increased risk of the investment. The first thing to ensure prior to considering exit or external investment is to ensure all financial matters are in order. This may require that you hire a CPA or accounting firm to vet your numbers.

- *Overview of the Business Model* – In this section, you should leverage your Business Model Canvas to convey to investors the details around your sustainable and repeatable business model. Use the BMC to list the key activities you provide and an explicit explanation of your value proposition to customers. Show evidence that customers agree with your value proposition hypothesis, and that the business model is sustainable long-term.

- *Product/Service Features* – This section will cover the specific details around your product or service and why it is valuable to customers. Identify the pain point you are solving for customers, describing in detail how your product or service meets your customers' needs.

- *Customer & Market Analysis* – Perform an objective competitive analysis on your market. Determine who your primary competitors are, and communicate the differentiating qualities of your product or service. Being objective and honest about your strengths and weaknesses in this section is crucial to gaining credibility with your potential investors. Glossing over major weaknesses will be seen through by sophisticated market participants, so best-practice is a straight forward and honest approach about both the strengths and weaknesses of your model.

- *Marketing & Branding* – In this section, you should highlight any marketing or brand value you have created since starting the business. An evaluation of repeat buyers, brand loyalty and marketing practices can help investors determine how you are positioned in the market.

- *Goals of Exit* – In this section, you should list the explicit goals you have set for your exit. If you are confident in your assessment of the valuation of your business, you could provide details in this section. Many entrepreneurs prefer to let the investors make the first move on valuation, so depending your situation you can make the determination on how transparent you wish to be on that front. Be succinct, and explain how a combination of your business and the investor will create synergies and value beyond the sum of the parts. If you can make a compelling case that the investor can bring crucial skills to the business and assist in its growth, the investor is more likely to see the investment in a positive light.

- *Conclusions* – Reinforce the most important points of the pitch. Provide performance highlights and explain why the company is well positioned for a sale.

Delivering a pitch can be stressful and complicated. Following this road map will allow you to objectively provide the details necessary to facilitate investment.

10.3: THE EXIT PROCESS

Exit Process: The exit process can get complicated, but it generally follows a prescribed process:

1. *Determine the need for exit* – The initial step in the exit process is deciding that you wish to exit. This decision is not made lightly, and may take months or years to reach. It is important to be realistic about valuation. Many entrepreneurs vastly overestimate how valuable their businesses are, and are disappointed when the market applies their own value to the business. Receiving a valuation from a third party can help provide a reality check for any entrepreneur.

2. *Begin the formal process of marketing your business for sale* – Once you have determined that an exit is likely, it is time to begin the formal process of marketing your business. This might involve engaging with an investment bank or financial intermediary to run your process, or you can choose to try and sell your business yourself. If you go it alone, be sure to engage high quality legal counsel to ensure your rights are being advocated for in the process.

3. *Pitch the business to prospective buyers* – During this time, you will be pitching your business to investors, answering data requests and providing responses to any inquiries from potential investors. Now, you might set up a "confidential data room" to hold your financial, strategic and operational materials. This data room may be password protected and shared with only a select group of identified targets.

4. *Receive LOIs from prospective buyers* – If your pitches are well-received, you will hopefully find interested parties who are willing to extend a non-binding letter of intent that indicates their genuine interest in evaluating an investment more fully. This step would officially kick off due diligence.

5. *Conduct due diligence to buyers' satisfaction* – Due diligence refers to a process where an investor will pore through your financials and supporting materials to ensure your representations in your pitch reflect reality. This process can be arduous and intense, but the better prepared you are to provide supporting materials, the more painless it will be.

6. *Identify the best offer* – If, after conducting due diligence, investors are satisfied with the state of the business, then it is time to pick the best offer. There are many considerations when comparing offers, which might include valuation, structure, involvement post-exit, board representation, who retains control of the organization, etc. Strong legal counsel is necessary to accurately interpret the deals on the table.

7. *Negotiate and execute the transaction* – After identifying your ideal acquirer, it is time to negotiate the final stages of the deal. This means creating official, binding documents that will build on the LOI and provide a framework for the deal.

Types of Exits: Various types of "exits" can be performed, based on how much control you are willing to part with and what role you wish to have in the company post transaction. Some entrepreneurs may be looking to retire, and could be satisfied with no involvement in the business after close. Others may wish to remain involved. Investors will sometimes require that a founder stays on for a transition period in order to smooth any bumps that the business might face during the process. The following types of exits are common in many industries

- *Acquisition by Larger Company* – Commonly, a large company will acquire a startup to add a brand, technology, intellectual property or another asset. The acquiring company will determine whether it is easier to buy it or build it.

- *Capital Investment* – Sometimes a group will make investments in existing businesses. They will either keep the existing management team, or provide new management. If an entrepreneur is tired of running a business and a private equity firm feels like new management could increase the value, then they may make an investment and the entrepreneur could be able to cash out.

- *Merger of Equals* – In a merger of equally sized entities, two companies that are roughly equivalent in size may become one, larger company.

- *Employee Buyout* – Employees are sometimes very interested in becoming owners when a founder is looking to move on. Unfortunately, employees are generally low on financial capital, so creative arrangements can be made to pass on ownership over time.

- *Succession* – A suitable successor may be a leading employee, heir, etc.

Types of Buyers: The most common types of investors are strategic and financial. In addition, some companies may be able to find a high net worth individual willing to invest in your business. The types of buyers your company may attract will depend on the success and size of your business, industry you operate within, stage of growth and ideal exit result.

- *Strategic Acquirers* - These are either public companies or large private companies and they will pay a premium if you have specialized technology, synergistic products, skilled employees, or a desired geographic location. They usually prefer to integrate the acquisition into their existing structure, and may insert their existing managers to improve the business. Strategic buyers focus on synergies and companies that can fit a hole in their offerings.

- *Sophisticated Financial Buyer* – These financial buyers generally manage large sums of money for high net worth individuals. They can be referred to as private equity or venture capital, depending on the stage. Private family offices, who manage the money of one person or family, are also involved in making investments in a broad range of industries. Financial buyers are more focused on good cash flow, a good management team in place, and good growth opportunities.

- *The Lifestyle Buyer* - Usually an individual looking for an income and the ability to build equity.

- *The Industry Buyer* - They usually approach you unsolicited and regard your company as vulnerable and inferior to their company. They are interested in select assets that they can buy at a discount.

10.4: SECTION QUESTIONS

1. What types of exits are most common? What type of exit appeals to you and why?

_____

_____

_____

_____

2. Who are the typical buyers for companies in your industry?

_____

_____

_____

_____

3. What about your company would make it attractive to an acquirer?

_____

_____

_____

_____

4. Name the steps of the exit process with a summary of each.

_____

_____

_____

_____

5. What are the key value drivers that an acquirer may consider?

_____

_____

_____

_____

CONCLUSIONS

Starting a business can be easy, but growing your business into something that can create value and support you is far more difficult. Many entrepreneurs are happy with small businesses that can provide for them and their families, but may never yield the large valuations or multiples that some companies harvest upon exit. A family restaurant owner, for example, may be happy simply working daily and growing his business. A technology startup, on the other hand, may be more interested in hitting a home run and create something that will be coveted by financial and strategic buyers.

In all of this, there is an intrinsic relation between the risks undertaken by businesses and their potential reward. Be sure that your goals and approach to starting a business mesh with your accepted risk tolerance. A mismatch can create issues and put incredible stress on an entrepreneur who is forced to take on more stress than they are comfortable with.

In the end, starting a business is a representation of the American Dream. You are taking control of your destiny and being brave in the face of uncertainty. It isn't a lifestyle that works for everyone, but for those that are fit for the role, it can be the most rewarding experience of their lives.

APPENDIX I: ENTREPRENEUR RESOURCES

This section will provide several valuable resources for potential and current entrepreneurs.

FIVE GREAT ENTREPRENEURIAL READS

This section will provide several valuable resources for potential and current entrepreneurs.

"Business Model Generation" *by Alexander Osterwalder*

One of the leading business model resources in the world, this book will further explain the intricacies and details of the Business Model Canvas (Buy on Amazon)

"4 Hour Work Week" *by Tim Ferriss*

Tim Ferriss has authored numerous books on health, fitness and entrepreneurship. His podcast is one of the most successful in the world. His 4HWW book has been on the bestsellers list of years and remains a bedside read for many entrepreneurs. (Buy on Amazon)

"Growth Hacking" *by Ryan Holiday*

Growth Hacking is a book that dives deeper into the tools and technologies necessary to succeed as an entrepreneur in the 21st century. Ryan has written several books, but this one is the most applicable to growing a business. (Buy on Amazon)

"Lean Startup" *by Eric Ries*

The Lean Startup is a cult classic amongst entrepreneurs, and discusses the various ways you can create a business on the cheap. A must read for anyone looking to get the most mileage out of every dollar invested.
(Buy on Amazon)

"Click Millionaires" *by Scott Fox*

This book focuses on the ways that you can make money leveraging the power of the internet. While not applicable to every business and situation.
(Buy on Amazon)

REVENUES	Budget 2017
Sale	
Cost of Goods Sold (COSGS)	
GROSS REVENUE	
Expenses	
Accounting	
Advertising & Promotion	
Insurance	
Legal and Professional Services	
Licenses	
Office Supplies	
Rent	
Salary	
Travel and Entertainment	
Utilities	
Miscallaneous	
TOTAL EXPENSES	

Earning before Tax (EBT)	
Taxes	
NET INCOME	

On the next page, *fill out the business model canvas as best you can. Don't be afraid to ask questions and work with each other to fill out each section!*

Key Partners

Who are our Key Partner?
Who are our key suppliers?
Which Key Resources are we acquiring from partners?
Which Key Activities do partners perform?

Key Activities

What Key Activities do our Value Propositions require?
Our distribution Channel?
Customer Relationships?
Revenue streams?

Key Resources

Why Key Resources do our Value Propositions require?
Our Distribution Channel?
Customer Relationships?
Revenue Streams?

Value Propositions

What value do we deliver to the customer?
Which one of our customer's problems are we helping to solve?
What business of products and services are we offering to each Customer Segment?
Which customer needs are we satisfying?

Customer Relationship

What type of relationship does each of our Customer Segments expect us to establish and maintain with them?
Which ones have we established?
How are they integrated with the rest of our business model?
How costly are they?

Channels

Through which Channel do our Customer Segment went to be reached?
How are we reaching them now ?
How are our Channel Integrated?
Who one's work best?
Which one's are most cost efficient?
How are we integrating them with customer routines?

Customer Segments

For whom are we creating value?
Who are our most important customer?

Cost Structure

What are the most important costs inherent in our business mode?
Which Key Resources are most expensive ?
Which Key Activities are most expensive ?

Revenue Streams

For what value are our customers really willing to pay?
For what do they currently pay?
How are they currently paying?
How would they prefer to pay?
How much does each Revenue Stream contribute to overall revenue?

ONLINE RESOURCES

There is a plethora of online resources and sites available to entrepreneurs. This represents a list that does not attempt to be exhaustive, but rather provides vetted options for a variety of needs.

The web is where most entrepreneurs live day to day. Email. Project management. Research. Spreadsheets. YouTube. Learning about the resources available to you is crucial to becoming a more educated entrepreneur. The list below is meant to provide an introduction to resources available.

OPERATIONS

- ThomasNET (www.thomasnet.com) – ThomasNet is an online consortium of contract manufacturers. No matter what you want to build. ThomasNET most likely has a company that you can contact. Contact manufacturers to validate costs and learn more about how products are made.

- Alibaba (www.alibaba.com) – Alibaba is an online marketplace that provides access to many manufacturers domestically and abroad. The site lists prices of many products without even needing to request a quote. Browse their lists or contact manufacturers through their platform to gain market / cost intelligence.

- GoDaddy (www.godaddy.com) – GoDaddy offers hosting and email services and is incredibly easy to use. If you are planning to manage your own website, GoDaddy can have WordPress installed on your new domain in under thirty minutes.

PRODUCTIVITY

- Hootsuite (www.hootsuite.com) – Manage your various social media accounts with a tool like Hootsuite, which allows you to schedule posts across multiple social channels at once, saving valuable time.

- Google Docs (www.google.com/docs/about) – Google Docs offers an easy way to share documents and files with coworkers. As your business grows and you add team members, you may outgrow the usefulness of Google Docs, but it is the most used tool of all entrepreneurs.

- Evernote (www.evernote.com) – Evernote allows you to catalogue and chronical notes via multiple mobile devices. Take a note on your phone that shows up on your iPad, etc. The functionality is easy to use, but robust enough to be useful as a business tool.

- Asana (www.asana.com) – Asana is a project management tool designed to help you keep everything straight.

- Basecamp (www.basecamp.com) – Coordinate workflows across multiple users to ensure everyone is on the same page.

ACCOUNTING & HR

- Zenefits (www.zenefits.com) – Zenefits provides basic HR services for free, allowing you to learn about how to stay compliant as you grow your business.

- Xero (www.xero.com) – Xero is a 21st Century born online accounting software package. Popular among entrepreneurs for its easy interface and slick features, Xero is a great option.

- QuickBooks (quickbooks.intuit.com) – QuickBooks has been around for ages and their online offerings are robust.

EDUCATION

- SlideShare (www.slideshare.net) – SlideShare (now owned by LinkedIn), provides educational decks and presentations from some of business' most influential voices. Search for any type of topic to learn more about it: marketing, strategy, how-to's of starting a business, etc. This is all provided free of charge.

- Quora (www.quora.com) – Quora is an online user group that answers questions of any kind. Experts chime in and answers are voted on by users, providing interesting reading if you have questions about certain aspects of entrepreneurship or business.

- 4 Hour Work Week Blog / Podcast (www.fourhourworkweek.com) – Tim Ferriss provides great resources for entrepreneurs including an informative blog with a vast archive of posts and a popular podcast.

- edX / Khan Academy / Coursera – There are plenty of websites that offer free courses in a variety of topics related to entrepreneurship. Search for any of the brands listed to find out if they offer classes you are interested in.

CodeAcademy (www.codeacademy.com) – So you want to learn how to code? CodeAcademy offers great courses in a variety of coding languages.

FREELANCE / CONTRACT RESOURCES

- 99Designs (www.99designs.com) – Provides a launching point for your brand at a reasonable cost. For less than $300, you can receive 30 logo options from highly qualified graphic designers. Options go up in benefit and cost from there.

- UpWork (www.upwork.com) – UpWork provides access to a vast array of freelance professionals, from legal to administrative. You can most likely find a resource on UpWork that has the skill set you are looking for. The entire financial exchange is managed by UpWork, removing stress from the relationship.

- Fiverr (www.fiverr.com) - Fiverr is known for offering services for as low as $5. This could be a quickly designed logo, someone with lots of followers shouting you out Twitter or someone writing a quick blog post.

This page left blank intentionally

This page left blank intentionally

This page left blank intentionally

Made in the USA
Columbia, SC
11 September 2021

45295710R00048